Best of the
Skagway Police Blotter
Vol. Two of an Alaskan Classic

also featuring
Heard on the Wind
Choice Comments from our Visitors

Welcome to my world! DAS

Best of the
Skagway Police Blotter
Vol. Two of an Alaskan Classic

also featuring

Heard on the Wind

Choice Comments from our Visitors

**Compiled and Edited
by Dave Sexton and Jeff Brady**

Cover Art by Kathy Cooney

**Lynn Canal Publishing
Skagway, Alaska**

Best of the Skagway Police Blotter

Vol. Two of an Alaskan Classic

also featuring

Heard on the Wind

Choice Comments from our Visitors

Copyright 2016 © by Lynn Canal Publishing
Dave Sexton and Jeff Brady, editors

All material in this book was previously printed in The Skagway News
under the editorship of publisher William J. "Jeff" Brady between 2005 and 2014.

Copies may be ordered from:
Lynn Canal Publishing
P.O. Box 498
Skagway, Alaska 99840-0498

Skaguay News Depot & Books direct line: 1-907-983-3354
www.skagwaybooks.com • store.skagwaybooks.com

ISBN: 978-0-945284-15-4

Distributed outside Skagway by Epicenter Press in the USA
and by PR Distributing in the Yukon/Canada

Table of Contents

Dedications

I faithfully believe that it is in the best interest of the community to know the activity of their police department, just as it is in the best interest of the police department for the community to know of their activity. To that end I have been writing police blotter entries for over 25 years. A couple of summers ago I was sitting in the lobby at the airport awaiting a flight. A summer resident was sitting with her parents who had apparently come to visit, and they were taking turns reading the blotter aloud from a current paper. I do not know where they were from, but it must have been a much more stoic place than Skagway as they were literally howling with laughter over the news. I was in my civilian attire so they had no idea I had written what they found so entertaining, but it was rewarding to me. I am thankful that even though we live and work in arguably the quietest and safest community in all of Alaska, I can still find tidbits now worthy of our second Skagway Police Blotter book. I am even more thankful that nowhere in the ten-year span recorded in this edition will you find antics attributed to my son, Walker, or daughter, Mackenzie! I dedicate my part of this book to them. – *Dave Sexton*

This book is also dedicated to Danny Brady, who spent seven years as a Skaguay Alaskan newsie during the period when most of the "Heard on the Wind" items herein were collected by his dad, "the windy one." Danny's "Extra! Extra!" could be heard loud and clear on the docks, and he now uses those vocal talents on Skagway High School's award-winning Drama, Debate and Forensics (DDF) team. – *Jeff Brady*

Acknowledgments

We are indebted to the hard work of Skagway police officers during the 10-year period that this volume covers and Police Chief Ray Leggett for giving Dave the leeway he needs to tell the stories in the blotter reports. As with our previous volume, half of the royalties are annually sent to the Skagway Police Services account to help with local programs like the Bike Rodeo and DARE. Thanks also to all who sent submissions for "Heard on the Wind."

Note to Readers

In putting together this second volume, we wanted to present it differently. Instead of organizing the chapters by subject, we decided to stick with the chronological order to show how police work in Skagway changes from winter to summer and back to winter. This also gives the reader a chance to follow certain story lines. There is a brief introductory summary at the start of each year's blotter. The "Heard on the Wind" chapters, which provide a break after every two years of blotters, are also organized in chronological order, but the only introduction needed for good wind was placed before the first chapter. The windy one says, "That's all you need. Enjoy!"

2005

The year begins with an unpaid bill and some vehicle crunches and ends with a threat of flooding from a warm weather front. In between, there were plenty of alcohol-related miscues downtown and on the roads and some puzzling thefts.

01/02/05: A Juneau hotel asked if SPD would contact a Skagway resident who left town before paying a $550 bill.

01/08/05: A victim reported to police that his pickup had been stolen from a State Street parking spot. Moments later a traffic collision involving the stolen truck and a vehicle parked on Main Street was called in. Police found the stolen truck had pushed the parked car 75 feet. Police arrested a 22-year-old Skagway man for Driving Under the Influence of Alcohol (DUI), driving while license suspended, and theft. The man blew a .256 BAC (Breath Alcohol Content).

01/22/05: Officer responded to a non-injury vehicle rollover accident on the Klondike Highway. Neither the 34-year-old Skagway resident nor her passenger was injured, however the 2003 GMC Envoy was considered a total loss.

02/05/05: Police and EMS personnel responded to a 911 call regarding a traffic accident with injuries. An intoxicated 32-year-old Skagway man fell off an ATV he was driving onto the intersection of Second and Broadway Street, where his intoxicated passenger left him, taking off on the vehicle back to the bar to call for help. The man was transported to the clinic by ambulance, and later charged with DUI and driving on a suspended driver's license.

Best of the Skagway Police Blotter

03/17/05: An officer responded to an airplane that was stuck on the runway with failed landing gear. The officer, who moonlighted as an airplane mechanic, was able to assist in the repairs and get the plane in motion again.

03/22/05: A 32-year-old Skagway man was arrested and charged with Harassment.

03/24/05: Police contacted two visiting teenage boys for blowing up garbage cans with fireworks.

03/31/05: A 54-year-old Juneau man was charged for being a convicted sex offender and failing to register with local police after moving to Skagway.

04/22/05: A gentleman reported a theft from his RV that was parked in Mountain View RV Park. As far as he can tell so far, items missing are a television, VCR, telephone, and a set of new jumper cables. When returning to Skagway this season, he found the motorhome wide open and knows it was locked when they left town last fall.

05/09/05: A black bear was dispatched after repeated attacks on chickens at a Dyea residence.

05/11/05: A 29-year-old seasonal resident was arrested on charges of attempted kidnapping, sexual assault and domestic violence.

05/15/05: A 60-year-old Skagway man was arrested for DUI after police received a call about a suspected intoxicated driver who had pulled into, and was now leaving Canadian Customs for the US. The man, who consented to a breath test indicating a BAC of .15, was cited and released.

05/16/05: A man hiking the Dewey Lake Trail thought he was lost and called 911. Dispatch was able to get him turned in the right direction, and he called later to advise he was back on the ship.

05/17/05: Dispatch received a complaint of a man urinating in public from the back deck of a downtown business.

05/20/05: A 56-year-old Oregon man was taken into emergency custody after he was found living in the woods in grave medical condition. The man advised he was homeless and had no means of financial support and was just "waiting to die." He was transported to Juneau for care.

2005

05/22/05: A resident reported the theft of a half a cord of wood from their yard.

05/24/05: A 37-year-old Juneau man was arrested for domestic violence assault, felony DUI, refusal to submit to a breath test, and driving on a suspended driver's license after police responded to a call for help at employee housing on Spring Street.

05/27/05: A 25-year-old Skagway woman was charged with misconduct involving a controlled substance for smoking marijuana in public.

05/28/05: Police responded to a call that someone unknown was trying to get into a residence where they did not belong on Broadway Street. Responding officers contacted an intoxicated 20-year-old seasonal worker from Mississippi. She was cited for with minor consuming alcohol and taken to her home on Third Avenue.

A black bear snoozes in the sun along the Klondike Highway near Tutshi Lake.

05/28/05: A 24-year-old Skagway man was cited for misconduct involving a controlled substance after police contacted him at his apartment on an unrelated matter and found him smoking marijuana inside.

06/02/05: Officers assisted removing a hornets nest from the school playground.

06/01/05: A water truck driver for a local contractor was cited for theft of water after he was found filling his truck from an unmetered hydrant.

Best of the Skagway Police Blotter

06/04/05: A 32-year-old Fairbanks man was arrested for DUI after police found him passed out behind the wheel of his vehicle with his foot on the brake. The man consented to a breath test indicating a BAC of .27, and he was cited and released.

06/16/05: Police stopped and arrested an 18-year-old Haines man bicycling on State Street for possession of a stolen handgun and violating his conditions of release (he was supposed to obey all laws while out). Also arrested was his highly intoxicated 21-year-old friend who disobeyed numerous requests not to interfere with his arrest. She was cited for disorderly conduct and released.

From right, Canadian Navy vessels HMCS Yellowknife and Whitehorse are flanked by the cruise ship Vision of the Seas, as the Nanaimo awaits its turn at the Ore Dock in June 2005. Members of the HMCS Whitehorse crew were taken north by the WP&YR to assist with the Yukon River Quest canoe race.

06/17/05: Police responded to a complaint of three underage drinkers walking down Broadway. Three Russian college students on a work exchange working at Westmark were contacted. All admitted to drinking alcohol, all were obviously under the influence, and all were cited and released.

06/19/05: Police contacted a 20-year-old seasonal worker having difficulty walking down Broadway at 2 a.m. The Colorado man was cited for minor consuming alcohol and taken home.

06/23/05: Police contacted a 20-year-old seasonal worker holding an open beer bottle downtown at 2 a.m. The Minnesota man was cited for minor consuming alcohol and released.

06/23/05: Officers and EMS personnel responded to an injured climber up the Klondike Highway. The man was later medevaced out for treatment.

2005

06/23/05: Officers and Fire personnel responded to a 911 call of tent on fire in an RV park. Fire was apparently caused by an unattended bug repellent candle.

06/28/05: A 28-year-old Anchorage man was taken into emergency custody and transported to Juneau for care after he was found naked and disorientated in a hotel room after ingesting a quantity of drugs and alcohol.

06/29/05: Police arrested a 40-year-old Ohio man on fugitive from justice charges. Franklin County, Ohio wanted the man on two counts of felony child neglect.

06/29/05: A highly intoxicated 46-year-old member of the Canadian Navy off of a Canadian Coast Guard vessel in port was arrested for Criminal Trespass after he refused to leave a bar when asked to do so by the bartender and a police officer.

07/01/05: Police arrested a 31-year-old Skagway man for disorderly conduct, violating the conditions of his release from a prior arrest, and giving false information to a police officer. An officer had responded to a disturbance at the Red Onion, and the intoxicated suspect identified himself as his twin brother, so he would not get in trouble for drinking and fighting in violation of the court order.

07/03/05: Police received a call from a victim who said she was chasing a bicycle thief atop her stolen bicycle toward the Railroad Dock. Police caught and arrested the 27-year-old seasonal worker, on charges of theft and possession of marijuana (found during the arrest process).

07/08/05: A 32-year-old seasonal worker was arrested for DUI after he was stopped for equipment and moving violations. The driver appeared obviously intoxicated to officers, and failed field tests when asked. He was cited and released.

07/12/15: A 29-year-old Skagway man was cited for being intoxicated in a licensed premise after he had been removed and warned by officers from each bar in town.

07/14/05: A 49-year-old Skagway man was arrested for DUI after officers watched his vehicle being operated recklessly around town. The man blew a .19 BAC and was cited and taken home.

07/16/05: A 21-year-old seasonal worker was arrested for sexual assault upon a co-worker at the workplace.

Best of the Skagway Police Blotter

07/18/05: A 50-year-old co-worker of the above was arrested on assault, witness tampering and hindering prosecution charges after she tried to convince the sexual assault victim to drop charges against the suspect.

07/21/05: It took all the way to Dyea for officers to catch and stop a speeding vehicle. The driver, a 42-year-old Willow resident, was cited for reckless driving, drinking while driving, speeding, open container, and no proof of insurance. She was given warnings for failure to carry a driver's license and failure to acquire an Alaska driver's license.

07/22/05: Police stopped a vehicle for poor driving and equipment problems and arrested the driver, a 33-year-old Skagway man, on charges of DUI and possession of marijuana. Due to his incapacitation he was held over for court.

07/22/05: A 24-year-old Romanian crewmember off the Sun Princess told police he lost control of his rental car when he drove through a thicket of alders and down a 12-foot embankment into Pullen Creek just off the Broadway Dock. Nobody was injured, and police estimate $6,000 damage to the vehicle, which was towed out. The driver was cited for negligent driving.

07/23/05: Twenty blasting caps were found on the Moore Creek Bridge on the Klondike Highway. Through traffic was stopped while the caps were recovered. The caps were safely detonated, and all appeared to be duds.

07/23/05: A 58-year-old Tennessee man was arrested for possession of a firearm while intoxicated and possession of a firearm on licensed premises after police received a complaint from patrons that he was carrying a .45 caliber handgun in the waistband of his pants while playing pool at the Bonanza.

07/24/15: A 38-year-old Toronto man was arrested for intoxicated person on a licensed premise, and criminal trespass after he refused a bartender's and officer's request to leave a bar at closing time.

07/27/05: A 27-year-old Oklahoma man was cited after he provided false information on a driver's license application. The man's privilege to drive is currently suspended in Oklahoma, and he is ineligible for a license.

07/28/05: Police arrested a 21-year-old seasonal worker for being an intoxicated person in a licensed premises after he refused several requests to leave a bar.

08/10/05: Police received a burglar alarm at the Trail Center. A responding officer found a blue BMX style bike lying on the ground at the back of the building and a fully opened window with the blinds down but crinkled. The officer and National Park Service rangers entered and cleared the building. Nobody was found inside the building, and the bicycle was confiscated.

08/10/05: A broken cash register containing $20 was taken overnight from a harbor-area store. The front door was closed but did not lock properly.

08/11/05: Police arrested a 41-year-old Skagway man for DUI after he was found passed out behind the wheel of a running vehicle in front of a tavern. After transport to the police department, he was also charged with refusing to take a breath test, possession of marijuana, and failure to register as a sex offender.

08/12/05: A 29-year-old seasonal worker with a history of self-inflicted injury was taken into emergency custody after he laid straight razors on a downtown bar and said he was going to kill himself.

08/16/05: A 47-year-old Sitka man was arrested on a Sitka warrant for felony assault and violating a domestic violence protection order.

Skagway patrolman Ike Lorentz pauses for a moment to talk with passersby on Broadway. The bike patrol was a new addition to the downtown scene during the summer of 2005.

08/16/05: Police cited a 17-year-old Skagway resident for possession of marijuana after her mother caught her smoking in the backyard

Best of the Skagway Police Blotter

08/19/15: Police arrested a 25-year-old seasonal worker for disorderly conduct after he created a disturbance by refusing to leave a bar when asked.

08/20/05: Police arrested a 24-year-old Skagway man for domestic violence assault after he threatened and scared his roommate.

08/21/05: Police investigated a complaint by a man who said he had been roughly escorted out of a bar by another patron.

08/21/05: Skagway officers assisted Juneau PD in locating a missing 24-year-old cruise ship passenger. The lady got off in Juneau, and did not get back aboard before the ship, which was now in Skagway, left port. Officers found a witness aboard who reported seeing the woman leave a Juneau bar with the bartender. She was located by JPD and flew to Skagway to rejoin her party.

08/21/05: Police arrested a 21-year-old Whitehorse man on burglary and theft charges after he stole a six pack of beer "on a whim after he saw the (alleyway) cooler door standing open" at the Red Onion.

08/22/05: Three cans of fruit were reported missing from a pantry shelf in a garage at a residence on Dyea Road.

08/23/05: An IBM Thinkpad laptop computer and Palm Pilot were reported stolen from baggage somewhere between the victim's ship and hotel. Loss reported to be around $1,700.

08/24/05: A residence at 20th and Main Street was reported entered and all of the lights turned on while its resident was away.

08/24/05: A 30-year-old highly intoxicated seasonal worker was held overnight for his own protection after police found him lying in the street in front of a bar. He was unconscious after another patron punched him once in the face after the downed man tried to start a fight.

08/25/05: After investigating the man who threw the above punch, officers tracked down the 24-year-old seasonal worker and arrested him for driving with a revoked license, failure to register as a sex offender in the state of Alaska, and misconduct involving a controlled substance after marijuana was found in his vehicle.

2005

08/27/05: Police arrested a 22-year-old highly intoxicated visitor from Ireland for disorderly conduct after they were called to the Westmark. Responding officers observed the man in a physical altercation with other guests who had asked him to turn his loud music down.

08/29/05: Police secured a search warrant and searched a Ninth Avenue residence a rifle used in an assault.

09/03/05: Police asked a party at 15th and Alaska to keep the noise down. Partiers advised they had been dancing in the yard to the Spice Girls, and celebrating the homeowner's last night in town.

09/03/05: Police arrested a 33-year-old local man for being an intoxicated person on a licensed premises and trespass after he refused several requests to leave a bar.

09/04/05: A small safe from the Stowaway Cafe containing an undisclosed amount of money was reported stolen sometime overnight. Police Chief Ray Leggett called it the worst burglary of the year. Officers recovered the safe the next day from Pullen Pond, however the door and cash were missing.

09/18/05: Police responded to a report of a fight at a downtown bar. Parties had been separated upon arrival, and nobody wanted to press charges. All went their separate ways after agreeing not to return.

11/02/05: A landlord called police and advised that a renter had moved out of a trailer but had left two live turkeys behind. For lack of a better idea, officer asked her to contact Paws & Claws animal shelter.

11/21/05: The city manager called to say that Lower Lake reservoir is at capacity. Somebody went up and moved some boards so that water would go into the spillway on top. If the water continues to rise it will come down right above Pullen Pond area. He asked that an officer keep an eye on the area tonight. Also, the Klondike Highway closed at 4 p.m. due to hazardous conditions, and a rock slide was partially blocking Dyea Road.

11/23/05: The Pullen Creek culvert area flooded as forecast above.

A view from the bridge of a cruise ship shows activity on the Railroad Dock as another ship disembarks passengers for the White Pass & Yukon Route train and other excursions.

2006

This was a very busy year filled with horses at play, mysterious home and bed invasions, errant bees and summer worker bees, dog car jackers, dumb criminals, an angry flightseeing passenger, and a murderous raven gang on the docks.

02/12/06: Report of two horses frolicking on highway. They were located and owners contacted.

03/03/06: A high schooler reported receiving death threats from another high schooler. Police counseled the suspect, and told her that while we probably did not need to know all of the details of their disagreement, it was illegal to make threatening phone calls, and she would have to desist in the making of them, or face the wrath of the law.

03/27/06: A Dyea Road resident reported she left her home unlocked while she was gone for a few hours, and returned to find drawers, cabinets and files rifled through. A couple of very cheap rings were missing, however an iPod, booze and expensive underwear were all left untouched. The home, locked this time, was entered again three days later. The back door was kicked in, and things were again gone through but not missing.

04/02/06: Officer responded to a report of a suspicious vehicle towing a 4-wheeler and forklift headed to Seven Pastures. Turned out to be authorized wood cutters.

04/04/06: Four tickets issued for vehicles blocking alleys and ignoring verbal warnings.

04/04/06: A 24-year-old State Street resident was cited for negligent driving after crashing into the Skagway River Bridge.

Best of the Skagway Police Blotter

04/20/06: A 42 year-old seasonal worker advised that he had gotten into a fight with a local woman last week, and that her "clan" had kicked the door to his room open last night and beat him up. He asked that officers contact his assailants and be told not to do it again.

04/24/06: A hotel manager reported that when he got to work today there was a room that had been slept in. To his knowledge the room was locked and person(s) broke in, made the bed, slept in it, and left prior to his arrival at 07:00 this morning. The hotel does not open until May 9.

04/26/06: A 34-year-old local woman was slightly injured when she had to lay her scooter down after an elderly driver pulled out in front of her on Broadway Street. He was cited for failure to yield the right of way.

05/02/06: Officer responded to a burglary in a downtown business. No signs of forced entry, but owner says the interior is not how he left it last winter. Approximately $200 cash and a small flat screen TV were reported missing.

05/12/06: A 40-year-old Skagway woman was taken into custody on an outstanding arrest warrant when she attempted to take a driving test. She paid the bail and was released.

05/18/06: Officer assisted local cruise line agents and the crew of the Norwegian Star with the removal of half a dozen passengers at the captain's request. Officers helped secure lodging for the passengers until they could be flown home the next day.

05/18/06: While shaking nighttime doors officers noticed a smoldering fire inside the Golden North. The fire was started by an improperly extinguished cigarette butt, and damage was contained to a scorched area of carpet. Responsible party responded to properly extinguish the fire, saving the oldest hotel in the state.

05/19/06: Police responded to a report of someone stuck on a cliff yelling for help near the Moore Bridge. The person was actually located near International Falls, and was helped out by motorists before rescue arrived.

05/20/06: Officers awoke and cited a Whitehorse youth for minor in possession of alcohol, after finding him sleeping on the grass in a yard on Broadway Street. He was turned over for safekeeping to friends camping in a RV park.

05/20/06: Officers responded to a disturbance at a local RV park. A trailer was heavily damaged during the melee, and the occupants were later evicted by the park manager.

5/21/06: Officers cited a 42-year-old Skagway man, who was about to become very familiar to officers, for driving on a revoked driver's license. Officers also confiscated his vehicle, until he could return with a valid driver.

05/22/06: An officer spotted sports equipment belonging to the school district on the Liarsville Road. When he took the equipment back, he found the school equipment room unlocked. The equipment was returned, and the room was checked and secured.

05/23/06: Police assisted in the death investigation of a passenger aboard the Dawn Princess. Police believe the death to be the result of natural causes.

05/23/06: A case involving a 42-year-old Skagway resident was forwarded to the District Attorney for possible charges. The man is believed to be a convicted sex offender who has failed to register as required. Record was found after the man was cited for driving while license revoked the day before.

05/25/06: Police received a found camera. The officer located a photo of the owner in the camera's memory that showed the photo had been taken from the Railroad Dock. The officer then showed the photo of the owner to the security chief of the Island Princess, who said he recognized the owner and could see that it was returned.

FISHING ON DUTY? – SPD Sgt. Ken Cox takes a few minutes out of a busy summer day to wet a line, though not for a fish. After dropping his patrol keys in the small boat harbor, he receives some help from father-in-law Dave Hunz and a magnet for his "catch of the day."
Photo submitted by Courtney Wilson

05/26/06: A restaurant reported that patrons kicked and damaged a door while exiting the building. Police contacted the suspect, and later were in turn contacted by the suspect's employer who advised that restitution and apologies would be forthcoming.

Best of the Skagway Police Blotter

05/30/06: Police received a complaint of alcohol and marijuana consumption occurring in the ball field dugouts next to the school. Officers will be making extra patrols in the area in an effort to curb this activity. The department would appreciate additional reports of ongoing nefarious activity in the area next to the school.

06/06/06: Police responded to a reported assault at Liarsville between employees. One man was transported to the clinic for stitches to an injury received via a baseball bat to the forearm.

06/08/06: Police investigated a non-injury traffic incident where a motorhome left the roadway for the ditch. The driver had reportedly been distracted by a bee in the vehicle.

06/08/06: Officers on foot patrol were beckoned by a shuttle following an intoxicated person who had caused a disturbance and broken a window out of the vehicle he was riding in. Officers jumped in the shuttle and followed the suspect vehicle until it stopped, where all the people inside were contacted and counseled before release.

06/08/06: Officers responded to a complaint of an illegal burn by a construction company on the Klondike Highway. Confirming the blaze was consuming hazardous materials, the fire department was summoned and extinguished the fire.

06/08/06: Police investigated a complaint of two men walking down Main Street smoking marijuana. Officers contacted the men, and watched one of them toss a joint on the road under the patrol car before approaching police. He said they were entertainers off a cruise ship, and voluntarily handed over the rest of the dope in his pocket and signed a ticket for possession rather than going through the hassle of being arrested.

06/08/06: Officers responded to a late night loud party complaint at employee housing on Spring Street. Party organizers were offered suggestions concerning minors consuming alcohol and noise that carries if they wanted to avoid undue police attention.

06/09/06: Officers received a complaint from a car owner who returned to her parked car to find it plastered with bumper stickers. The residents of the house she had parked in front of did not approve of anyone other than themselves parking in front of their residence, and papered the offending vehicle. The Department wishes to remind residents that while it may seem impolite to park in front of a house

14

that's not your own, the public streets belong to everybody, and drivers are free to park in any unregulated spot they find open.

06/15/06: Minor vandalism was reported at the small boat harbor when several skiffs were found untied and floating around the harbor, in addition to a cart and some bicycles thrown into the water.

06/16/06: A driver made the error in judgment of yelling and waving a beer can at an officer on foot patrol as he sped past. A second officer out and about in his patrol car stopped the suspect vehicle and recovered two empty beer cans and an empty malt liquor bottle from the two 18-year-old occupants. Both were cited for minor in possession of alcohol, as well as the driver also being cited for driving after consuming.

06/17/06: Officers stopped a vehicle for expired registration tabs and no brake lights. The driver was unaware of these conditions, as he had just "stolen" the vehicle from a co-worker, and was in the process of hiding it.

06/18/06: Just after midnight officers watched a small car unload six young adults into the cemetery on the Dyea Road just off the Klondike Highway. Officers contacted them after they exited the cemetery. The youths explained they had been trying to scare friends who were camping overnight among the graves. All were sent home.

06/20 – 06/22/06: Police unlocked three vehicles for owners who had left dogs inside the vehicle. The dogs locked each of the owners out.

06/23/06: Police recovered what they believed to be a missing dog. Turned out it was another missing dog that had not yet been reported missing. Dog #2 was returned to owner and officers continued to look for dog #1.

6/24/06: Police received a 911 call from a pay phone here in town – the caller advised he didn't know who or where he was. Officers were able to identify him as a Haines resident with mental health issues, and EMS took him back to Haines on the fire rescue boat.

06/24/06: Officers arrested the 42-year-old sex offender for violating his conditions of release by consuming alcohol after he was observed inside the beer garden at the summer solstice party. He was held overnight awaiting a visit with the magistrate.

Best of the Skagway Police Blotter

06/26/06: Police and Fire responded to a report of a missing picnic table, a campfire built under the picnic shelter, fire damage to one of the shelter pilings, and an active fire in the ring outside the shelter at Smuggler's Cove.

06/29/06: Police identified two men doing a hatchet job on a 20-foot-long log of down cottonwood. They were told White Pass didn't like people walking on their property, so it would be officer's best guess they didn't like people chopping on their property either. Lumberjacks were told if White Pass wanted to push the issue they'd be back.

Visitors get on a bus marked 'Wrong Coach" on the Railroad Dock.

06/30/06: Police investigated a reported large party scheduled for Smuggler's Cove. Police found a pyre of wooden pallets awaiting sacrifice, and told party planners they were not allowed anything larger than a small cook fire.

06/30/06: Police received a report of a possible plane crash on Dewey Peaks. An officer spoke to the witness, who believed he could see a plane resting on the scree slopes. Although the officer scanned the area with binoculars, he was unable to locate what the visitor thought he saw.

06/30/06: An officer temporarily halted a softball game at the school ballfield after observing mass drinking of intoxicants by players and spectators despite warning signs to the contrary. Over four dozen cans or bottles were dumped in the field Dumpster as a result of the intervention before play resumed.

07/01/06: An officer responded to a report of a possible intoxicated driver swerving on State Street. Turned out to be a visitor gawking at the sights.

2006

07/03/06: Officers charged a 21-year-old Skagway man with DUI after they investigated a non-injury traffic collision on Broadway Street. Major disabling damage was inflicted onto the suspect vehicle and a parked pickup, with minor damage incurred on a third vehicle. Subject was transported to the department where he consented to a breath test resulting in a .07 BAC and released on his promise to appear for court.

07/05/06: After a dog, possibly scared by fireworks, jumped aboard her bus at the Ore Dock, a SMART bus driver delivered it to the police department. Officers were able to reunite the roaming dog with owner. The bus driver did not charge the dog a fare.

07/06/06: A Fifth Avenue business reported an overnight burglary in which $70 was missing. Police developed a suspect in a man who the day before said he had no money and was looking for food. Apparently the man had left town after purchasing a $48 ticket on a 4:30 a.m ferry to Haines.

07/07/06: Our 42-year-old suspected sex offender was charged with violating the conditions of his release (again) after officers on patrol observed him leave a downtown bar after consuming intoxicants (again).

07/08/06: Officers charged a 49-year-old Craig man with DUI after he was stopped for negligent driving. Subject was transported to the department where he consented to a breath test resulting in a .21 BAC and released on his promise to appear for court.

07/12/06: Police investigated the death of a 20-year-old Maine man who fell during a guided climbing trip. Cause of death determined to be a pre-existing condition and not the result of the fall.

07/14/06: Police received a 911 call from a man who stated there was a drunk sleeping in the stairwell of his apartment building. An officer contacted the sleeping man, who could not find his pants or shoes and could not remember anything after he left the Red Onion. He was given a ride to his residence 13 blocks away.

07/14/06: Princess Tours reported a bear at the Dyea Road overlook hanging out pretty close to the tour bus. Responding officers fired three cracker rounds and sounded their siren until the bear left for the woods.

Best of the Skagway Police Blotter

07/14/06: Patrolling officers discovered that many traffic signs on the Dyea Road were shot up overnight by a combination of handgun, rifle and shotgun rounds.

07/15/06: Canada Customs turned back a vehicle with an Alaska license plate in the back seat and were told to report to Skagway Police. The two ladies aboard told police that they found it. They were told it is illegal to keep something that doesn't belong to you, and returned it to the Skagway registered owner.

07/22/06: A 28-year-old Skagway man found passed out behind the wheel of a vehicle parked but running on Broadway Street was charged with DUI. Subject was transported to the department where he consented to a breath test resulting in a .16 BAC and released on his promise to appear for court.

07/26/06: Police investigated the apparent death by natural causes of a 54-year-old Kansas man aboard a cruise ship.

07/26/06: Police responded to a domestic disturbance on Alaska Street, however was unable to locate the suspect, the 42-year-old sex offender from prior calls. Police however did seek and receive a warrant for his arrest on two charges of assault (for his girlfriend and his girlfriend's mother) and did locate and arrest him the next day.

07/27/06: Police investigated a flightseeing helicopter crash approximately 14 miles from town. The helicopter was destroyed, however the passengers aboard suffered only minor injuries.

07/28/06: Skagway and Haines police investigated a possible child neglect case involving a 10-year-old Skagway youth being sent to the SE State Fair in Haines for the weekend on her own.

07/30/06: Officers received a complaint from one food vendor complaining about another repeatedly checking her out – for possible food-handling violations. She asked that he be warned about possible trespassing or harassment violations.

07/30/06: A U.S. Border Protection officer referred to Skagway Police a man from Juneau attempting to enter the U.S. with a reportedly stolen license plate on his vehicle. Officers took the plate off the vehicle, and referred the man to Juneau PD for follow-up.

2006

07/30/06: A 27-year-old Skagway man was cited for driving on a suspended driver's license, reckless driving, and leaving the scene of an injury traffic accident after police responded to an aid call and report of a single car accident on Dyea Road. The driver, who passengers said was doing at least 60 in a 25 mph zone before crashing, fled the scene prior to police arrival and had to be tracked down and arrested.

08/02/06: Two Skagway men, age 22 and 28, were arrested on charges of burglary and assault after they reportedly broke down the door of a 27-year-old man's apartment and beat him. Both were transported to the State Prison at Lemon Creek.

08/03/06: A 25-year-old Alabama man was cited by police for driving while license suspended. The man had been turned around by Canadian Customs for driving a vehicle adorned with license plates not registered to that vehicle. The (expired) plates that did belong on that vehicle were found hidden inside the vehicle. It is believed the plates on the car were stolen in Juneau.

08/04/06: Officers escorted a driver down the Klondike Highway after she felt she could not make it to town by herself in the fog.

08/07/06: A camper complained that when she had asked the owner of a dog that was howling to quiet the dog, the owner of the dog and his friends started to howl also. All was quiet when police responded and checked the area.

08/09/06: Police responded to a complaint of a fight among train passengers. After the train returned to the depot officers contacted the parties involved, who advised the incident consisted of yelling and some minor finger poking, and declined to press charges.

08/11/06: Police filed charges against a Juneau couple for knowingly providing a vehicle to their son, a Skagway summer resident (who crashed his car 07-30) who has had his privilege to drive revoked, suspended or canceled 12 times since 1995, and allowing him to drive.

08/13/06: Police were dispatched to a report of a suspicious looking person lurking around the downtown area "watching the girls go into the Red Onion." Responding officers advised that he looked suspicious, because he was the only man downtown not wearing a pushup bra and dress, and that nobody should have to work the RO Drag Night. He was watched for a while, however officers saw nothing that separated him from the crowd.

Best of the Skagway Police Blotter

08/14/06: Officers arrested a 38-year-old Juneau man on an outstanding federal arrest warrant for wire fraud. He was held overnight and picked up the next day by U.S. Marshals.

08/15/06: Officers arrested a 27-year-old Juneau woman on an outstanding state arrest warrant for failure to appear. She was transported to Juneau.

08/17/06: A burglary involving the theft of $40 worth of food taken from a residence at 11th and Broadway Street was reported. The thief entered the house through a sliding glass door in the middle of the night while the residents were asleep. Turned out to be a family member who had been "kicked out of the house."

08/22/06: A Dyea Road resident reported that one can each of peaches, apricots and fruit cocktail were taken from the pantry cabinet in his unlocked garage.

08/24/06: Police received five calls in five minutes complaining of a loud fight at Sixth and Main Street. Half of the argument had fled before the officer arrived, the other half agreed the fight was over and to desist in disturbing the neighborhood.

08/26/06: Police separated combatants from a bar fight that had poured into the street. One half told police the next day that the other half had broken into his bedroom after the fight and threatened him with a gun. Police searched the suspect's residence with a warrant and found an armory but not the weapon described.

08/26/06: Police investigated the death of a cruise ship passenger who apparently died of natural causes between Juneau and Skagway.

09/03/06: Police, Fire and EMS responded by vehicle and helicopter to a serious work train derailment on the Canadian side of the border between Log Cabin and Bennett, BC. The injured and one fatality were transported to Whitehorse, and the investigation was handled by RCMP.

09/05/06: Officers responded to a report of a yelling woman lying on the boardwalk. The woman was not feeling well, and wanted a taxi back to her cruise ship. Officers arranged for same.

09/05/06: A store clerk called police after a ship's crew member took a jacket worth $200. The thief passed a backpack containing the jacket off to another crewmember at Pullen Park, and the clerk had this second person detained. Officers arrived and searched the backpack, which also contained $50 worth of crystal taken from another store, and a $130 stereo taken from a third. Police were unable to locate the original thief. The second man was turned over to U.S. Customs and Border Protection officers. The merchandise was returned to the stores.

09/05/06: Officers responded to a disturbance at Sixth and Main Street and arrested a 25-year-old Skagway man for misdemeanor DV assault involving his sister.

09/06/06: An employer found and turned over to police a burnt spoon and cotton ball (suspected heroin) left in a restroom. The suspect/employee fled to Canada before police could question him.

09/08/06: Police responded to an altercation at a downtown bar. The suspect was gone on officer's arrival. Police secured an arrest warrant the next day, and picked up a local 27-year-old Skagway man on charges of assault and violation of conditions of release on prior reckless driving and leaving the scene of an accident charges. He was released on $5,000 bail.

09/08/06: Police arrested the suspected 32-year-old heroin user upon returning from Canada on an outstanding arrest warrant. He was released on $4,100 bail.

09/10/06: Chilkat Guides reported spotting a pickup that had run over the embankment and into a tree at about 2.5 mile Dyea Road. Officers investigating the accident learned that the vehicle had been stolen the night before from in front of a downtown bar. The vehicle suffered major damage. An intoxicated man with possible broken

In an incident that did not make the blotter, "Professional Squirrel Abatement Specialist" Karen Briner successfully relocated "loquacious and bodacious" squirrels from the Railroad Dock to the Gold Rush Cemetery on Aug. 6. "All went well and no squirrels were harmed in the process, but my cat carrier is pretty messed up." Alas, it was reported that a squirrel had made the two-mile journey back to the dock after a few days.

ribs and no good way of explaining them presented himself to the clinic the next day for care.

09/18/06: Police were called to the airport to help with a woman who was very angry that she did not get a window seat on a helicopter flightseeing trip. When she came back into the building she threw a fit and started kicking the building and ranting, and was now refusing to leave. Officers took the woman into custody, and transported her back to her cruise ship. No charges were filed.

09/21/06: Police responded to a five-suspect fight that had spilled out of downtown establishment and into the street. Nobody wanted to press charges, all were sent home.

09/24/06: Police investigated another assault that had spilled out of the same establishment and onto the same street.

09/27/06: The police chief and harbormaster, using the city's rescue boat, picked up four men stranded at Burro Creek after their boat's engine failed.

10/02/06: AP&T found six pairs of sneakers tossed over the wires near employee housing on Alaska Street. One pair of shoes was signed with the name of its owner. The bucket truck was used to take the shoes from the wires. Officers contacted the employer of the suspects and advised that AP&T would be sending him a bill for the use of the bucket truck to remove the sneakers.

10/06/06: Officers coned off an area around a car-sized boulder that had fallen from a cliff wall and onto a jersey barrier, jutting partially out into the Klondike Highway.

10/07/06: Police investigated a burglary to a State Street business. Suspect(s) smashed a window to gain entry during the night. Rolls of quarters were taken.

10/08/06: Police received a complaint of a burglary to a State Street residence in which someone kicked in the front door and defecated in the hallway. Nothing else appeared disturbed inside; officers were unable to locate any neighboring witnesses.

10/10/06: Public Works crew recovered two vehicles that had been abandoned in the brush near West Creek. Officers tracked down the last known operator, who agreed to be billed for the recovery.

10/11/06: Police investigated an apparent at home death from natural causes of a Dyea resident.

2016

10/16/06: Officers attempted to aid school personnel and parents with teen age boys who are making it a habit to fight after school. Intervention is continuing.

10/17/06: Police, Rescue and Harbor personnel in Skagway and Haines searched for Skagway residents overdue from a fishing trip. They were located, OK, in Haines.

10/19/06: Police responded to a fight at a downtown establishment. Officers transported the victim to medical care for a deep laceration to the head and a chipped tooth. Police sought and received an arrest warrant for a 32-year-old assault suspect who had fled the scene (same suspect who fled to Canada over heroin earlier) prior to the officers' arrival. He turned himself in on Oct. 23 and was released after posting $1,000 bail.

10/23/06: Police investigated a loud music complaint coming from a residence off State Street. Officers located the source, and could see through a window a resident inside sleeping on the couch in front of the neighborhood-offending stereo. Unable to wake the resident, the officers entered the home, turned down the stereo, and left a business card atop the slumbering resident.

10/27/06: Police received a call from the harbormaster advising that he had removed a ladder from a derelict vessel housed in the shipyard for the second time. It is unknown if people are exploring or scavenging onboard. He said he would post the ship against trespassing and asked police to keep an eye on it.

10/29/06: A Main Street resident reported that someone broke into her residence and stole almost $3,000 in cash, approximately 10 DVDs, and a pair of pink sandals.

11/02/06: Police received a call from a man who had departed the ferry in Haines without retrieving a bag containing prescription narcotics and opiates. An officer retrieved the bag from the ferry cart in Skagway, and had it flown back to Haines.

11/11/06: Officers cited a 36-year-old Skagway man for possession of marijuana and a pipe used for smoking same. He had been contacted after police received a complaint of drug sales at a residence on Alaska Street.

Best of the Skagway Police Blotter

11/21/06: Several bomb threats to the airport were e-mailed to a local business. Police checked with the FBI who advised they were receiving the same complaint all over the state and nationwide.

11/29/06: Officers checked the Klondike Highway for an overdue motorist.

12/01/06: Two construction workers rescued a small owl that was being attacked by ravens down at the dock. They turned it over to the police, who contacted the raptor center in Sitka for advice. Staff tried to care for the owl, however it later expired.

12/03 to 12/05/06: A Long Bay resident reported the theft of 50-70 gallons of fuel oil from his cabin's storage tank. A 22nd Avenue resident later complained of having a half of a tank of gasoline siphoned from his vehicle and something crammed in the gas tank fill spout while he was out of town.

12/06/06: A Main Street resident told police she was surprised when an unknown male opened her front door and walked into her house. She yelled at him, and he ran away.

12/09/06: An officer responded to the U.S. Border Station where agents had contacted a vehicle containing an open alcohol container and a small amount of marijuana. An occupant was cited and refused entry.

Heard on the Wind

Curious questions and comments posed by visitors to Skagway

The popular Skagway News column "Heard on the Wind" was introduced during the 1999 visitor season after someone asked the news staff why we didn't print the crazy questions asked by our visitors. It made good sense and the column became an immediate "go to" spot in the paper, along with the blotter. The editor later began calling himself "the windy one."

The first "Heard on the Wind" entry came from a visitor asking about a sluice box display in the window of Richter's that worked like a fountain: "Is that water real?"

– May 28, 1999

And the questions became even more curious as the summer progressed:

"When do you people celebrate Christmas here?" – 06/09/99

"Is this the same river we cruised up on?"
– 06/25/99

"What time is it? Is that Skagway local time?" – 07/09/99

"Look, a hummingbird! Do their wings ice up in the winter?" – 08/13/99

"Is Skagway also known as Dawson City?"
– 09/19/99

Skagway kids line up outside the Kone Kompany on Broadway for the annual opening of the ice cream store in early May, a local ritual that tells us the summer season is about to begin.

25

HEARD ON THE WIND

A 100-year-old headline in the centennial edition of the Skaguay Alaskan visitor newspaper barked, "Skagway Is The Only Real City in Alaska." It prompted this response from a visitor, "But we were just in Juneau. Isn't that a city?" (Actually Juneau was incorporated a day after Skagway in June 1900).
– 05/26/00

A man in line at the post office complained: "I can understand them wanting to keep this place looking like it did 100 years ago, but $3 for a beer?!" – 06/09/00

"Was the gold rush seasonal?" – 06/23/00

A visitor looking out the window of her train at the forest asked, "Why do you plant your trees so close together?" – 07/09/00

A woman came into a store looking for Native-made moccasins. After she was taken to them, she asked, "Do they come in heels?" – 08/25/00

Another visitor asked, while inspecting some fossilized ivory art, "Were any mammoths harmed in the gathering of this ivory?" – 09/08/00

After being told to look out for northern lights on a rare, clear September night, a visitor said, "We'll be in Haines tonight. Do they run the show over there too?"
Another chimed in: "Can you see the northern lights when the ship is in port?" 09/22/00

A newly arrived visitor off the ship was overheard on Broadway: "I couldn't tell where we were on the cruise up here. There were no signs along the way." – 05/21/01

When asked in the bookstore if they carried any Native American stories, the clerk replied, "Yes, we have Tlingit, Haida and Athabaskan stories."
The woman replied, "No, I want Native American stories." – 06/22/01

Sometimes, it's the locals who get it wrong. When a visitor asked a local store clerk if the mountainside was covered in birch and Sitka spruce, the clerk replied: "Oh no, we're a long way from Sitka. Those are Skagway spruce." – 07/13/01

HEARD ON THE WIND

Early one damp morning by the visitor center, a small herd of visitors came up to the editor and asked, "Are we in Juneau or Fairbanks?"

After being told they were in Skagway, one asked, "How far is town anyway? Gosh, you can hardly see it." – 08/10/01

A tour operator was asked, "How old does a deer have to be before you call it a moose?" – 08/24/01

A customer, who may have been from Georgia by his accent, asked a clerk at the grocery store, "Y'all have ice?"

"Yep."

"Is it froze?"

Another customer complimented a clerk for speaking "very good English for having lived here such a long time." – 09/14/01

A cruise ship entertainer said they had a problem with a passenger in the early morning hours. The ship had made an announcement that there were "whales at three o'clock." Instead of running to the starboard side of the vessel to check the action, one passenger went to his room and set his alarm for 3 a.m. He was quite upset with crew when he got up and complained loudly about not seeing any whales. – 09/14/01

A moose and a polar bear from a cruise ship take a break from posing for photos and read the Skaguay Alaskan visitor newspaper, which uses the 1897-1898 gold rush spelling of the town.

Two visitors were walking down Broadway and puzzled by the tour seller on the corner. "What's that guy doing, scalping tickets?" – 09/28/01

While passing through a train at the start of a Summit Excursion trip, greeting passengers, a man looked up and asked the conductor, "Is she (the narrator's voice coming over the public address system) going to talk throughout the entire trip? I didn't come to Alaska to be educated." OK, the conductor thought, to each his own. Minutes later while returning to the coach, he noted that most passengers in this coach, including the complaining fellow, wore name tags. Upon inspection, he saw they were part of an Elderhostel educational group!– 05/17/02

HEARD ON THE WIND

A newsie handing out Skaguay Alaskans down at the Broadway Dock was asked by a visitor who edited the paper. "The publisher," the newsie replied.

"He spelled Skagway wrong," the visitor said, unaware that the 1897-98 spelling was with a "U."
– 05/17/02

A guard at the border station reported that, on a particularly foggy morning, an old lady pulled up in a white Cadillac, and asked: "Why'd you all build that damn road in the fog?" - 05/31/02

And what about this intruder alert...
A local store owner walked down the hall in her private residence only to find a tourist standing outside a locked bathroom door. When the resident asked the lady what she was doing, she replied that her friend had an emergency and was using the bathroom. The resident responded that she was in a private residence. The tourist responded, " I know but it was an emergency"! – 07/26/02

Seeing is believing...
At the Days of '98 show ticket counter, one woman asked about the Robert Service poetry recitation.
"Is Robert Service really going to be here?"
Upon finding out that he was dead, she said, "But I saw his books." - 08/23/02

It's summertime, the fish are jumping and the fireweed is high...
A lady was looking across Summit Lake with binoculars and commented on all the fish jumping.
The tour guide asked where.
"All over, there are hundreds of them," she replied.
The tour guide took one look and said, "Ma'am, those are white caps!" - 08/23/02

Please look at a map...
A woman came into the visitor center and asked if Skagway was connected to Sitka by a road.
"No, most islands in Southeast aren't connected to the mainland by roads," she was told.
"Sitka is an island?!" exclaimed the woman.
"Yes, Baranof Island," was the reply.
"Does that mean it has water on all sides?" asked the woman. - 09/13/02

2007

Errant pick-ups driven by the unlicensed, crazy cats on Broadway, tips on the fly, pizza by the pie, dog rescues, thieves caught on camera, stray bears and even porcupines downtown.

01/08/07: Police had numerous contacts over several days with a disruptive Canadian couple and their disabled (later abandoned) vehicle.

01/15/07: RCMP asked the department to attempt to locate the Canadian couple from above, check her welfare as she may be being held against her wishes, and seize a stolen vehicle he may be driving. Officers were unable to locate the pair, who later turned up in Prince Rupert.

01/26/07: Industrial explosives, possibly left behind from the Dyea Road widening project, were found on the beach at Long Bay. Police turned them over to a local explosives handler for destruction.

01/29/07: An Idaho woman asked police to contact an apparently intoxicated Skagway man who had placed late night calls to her or her father over three dozen times. She believes the man had at one time dated her sister. A dispatcher was able to contact the man and asked him to cease and desist the calling.

02/08/07: A local craftsman received threats from a mail order customer regarding a billing snafu.

02/08/07: While on patrol police observed a man leaving a local drinking establishment and head toward a parked car, however the man took off when he noticed the patrol car. Officers checked the car, which had expired plates, and discovered the registered owner had a criminal history of delivering con-

Best of the Skagway Police Blotter

trolled substances, assault, resisting arrest, DUI, and disorderly conduct. Officers did not locate the driver, nor had any further problem.

02/11/07: A caretaker reported two open windows on houses he was watching, and asked for an officer to assist in checking for trespassers.

02/26/07: A $700 welding torch and a pair of tennis shoes of unknown value were reported stolen out of a disabled vehicle left at Fourth and Main.

03/01/07: A Fifth Avenue employee reported her pickup truck that she had parked near State Street was missing when she returned to it after work. Police searched town, and located it abandoned on 22nd Avenue near Alaska Street. The pickup, with keys still in the ignition, was apparently unharmed.

03/04/07: Police were dispatched to 11th and State Street, after witnesses were awoken in the wee hours when a dark-colored pickup crashed into a parked car and then fled the scene. Officers successfully searched the town for the suspect vehicle and later charged a 22-year-old Sitka man with first degree vehicle theft, DUI, driving while license suspended, leaving the scene of an accident, and an outstanding arrest warrant from Sitka for probation violation. He was remanded to the Lemon Creek Correctional Facility in Juneau on $10,000 bail.

03/06/07: Police attempted to assist a local resident who was locked out of a borrowed vehicle. The ignition key did not work on the doors.

03/08/07: Police assisted a distraught mother with contacting her son whom she hadn't heard from in over a year and half. Son is now a resident of Skagway and will call his mother.

03/11/07: Police were dispatched to Third and Main Street, after witnesses called regarding a dark pickup with a snowmobile in the back crashing into a parked car and then fleeing the scene. Police back-tracked the vehicle to see where it had come from, and found the driver of the vehicle just completing a call to the owner of the other vehicle. No citation was issued.

03/17/07: Police responded to an altercation reported at Fourth and Main Street. One of the participants of the altercation was sent to the clinic for medical care. The other participant was passed out drunk and was transported home. No charges were filed.

03/23/07: A local B&B owner reported the theft of a piece of artwork from the business.

03/27/07: A report of a stolen vehicle was received. An officer was on his way to check it out when the vehicle was seen driving down Main Street. The driver was not the thief but a friend of the owner. The driver was aware of the missing vehicle, and when he saw it parked on the street, he drove it back to the owner.

04/24/07: A Broadway Street man reported his neighbors had been involved in a domestic dispute. He said he doesn't know their names, but the man hit his girlfriend and then threw a knife out the window. The caller now has the knife. Police investigated and arrested a 23-year-old Skagway woman for assault.

04/30/07: Police responded to a report of a child locked in a vehicle. Vehicle was opened successfully.

05/01/07: Police attempted to apprehend a crazy cat that was wreaking havoc on Broadway. Cat, in its attempt to evade capture by the NPS, bit and scratched its way loose. NPS employee is going to the clinic to have his injuries treated.

OOPS – A sailboat runs aground in the Small Boat Harbor during the 2007 summer season.

05/01/07: Police responded to a report of trespassing in one of the NPS buildings. The door to Soapy Smith's Parlor on Second Avenue was broken and it is suspected that someone slept there last night.

05/13/07: An officer was approached by a visitor who advised that he had given one of his two dogs away – and his wife was not very happy about it and he needed the dog back. He did not however know whom he gave the dog to. Officer advised without someplace to start we probably couldn't be much help finding the new owner.

Best of the Skagway Police Blotter

05/14/07: A vehicle with a flat tire left on a residential driveway on Dyea Road was reported missing. Police located it at employee housing off the Klondike Highway, and found two residents who heard it pull up around midnight the night before.

05/16/07: Police responded to a theft report from a downtown business. Officer spoke to suspect, who then returned the merchandise.

05/23/07: Police received a complaint that a food item had been purchased from a local market and the expiration date was January 2007. He was advised to take the item back for a refund or exchange.

05/24/07: Police responded to a complaint that a cruise ship member had shoplifted a pair of sandals and two jackets. Officers located the suspect on board ship and recovered the merchandise. Customs officers were contacted and they revoked his I-95 (privilege to leave ship). Items were returned to store.

05/25/07: A three-foot-square Alaska themed quilt with moose on it was reported missing from an AB Hall restroom where it had been hanging on the wall.

05/28/07: Police were called to assist at the clinic with a heavily intoxicated man who rode his bicycle into the stream near Eighth and Broadway. Police stayed while a gash over his eye was stitched up, and then gave the man a ride home.

05/28/07: Police assisted an NPS ranger in checking out the "Old Miner's Meat Market" across from the Fire Hall, where a door lock had been broken.

05/31/07: Police received a report from a visitor to Skagway that he had parked his vehicle in the West Creek area. He said that upon return, the back and side windows were broken out of his vehicle. Two rocks were found inside the cargo area of his vehicle.

05/31/07: Police responded to a disturbance between an angry customer and a tour operator. Customer was advised that officers could not help her with a price dispute, however if she continued to scare away clientele she was subject to arrest.

05/31/07: Police responded to a call of a man riding a bicycle on the airport runway, and contacted a pilot. He was searching for a tip that he was given by one of his passengers. The wind blew it out of his hand and he was trying to retrieve it.

2007

06/01/07: Police responded to a complaint of a man yelling and screaming. Man was found passed out in the street and tried to fight police after they woke him up. After he calmed down, he was released to a sober adult.

06/03/07: A loose dog was struck and killed by a passing train near the Gold Rush Cemetery.

06/04/07: Officer responded to a disturbance at a store. Customers were arguing about who was first in line.

06/05/07: Cash totaling $627 was found on Second Avenue and turned over to police, who tracked it down to a bus company.

06/06/07: Customers of a tour company requested to speak to an officer. While on a tour they had been in a motor vehicle accident with an injury. The tour guide did not contact the police department, and was apparently hoping his passengers wouldn't either. Police contacted company management.

06/15/07: A man claimed he ordered only a slice of pizza with two toppings on it, but he received a whole pizza instead. He claimed that he did not have to pay for it because it was the waiter's fault for not listening. A review of the menu showed the pizza was not available by the slice. He paid and left.

06/15/07: At 10:05 p.m., a citizen called reporting that he found a six-year-old boy out wandering around. Dispatch called parent, who was already out looking for the child.

06/16/07: Officer responded to a call that a dog was in the water by the ferry terminal and was unable to get out up the rock embankment. With assistance from Fire Dept. and climbing gear, the dog was rescued.

06/17/07: A 38-year-old Big Lake man stopped a park ranger along Dyea Road and inquired about watching seals. The ranger noticed open beer containers in the vehicle and an odor of intoxicants. The ranger called officers, who arrested and charged the man for DUI after he provided a breath sample resulting in a .10 BAC.

06/19/07: A 50-year-old Yukon man was arrested for assault in the fourth degree by National Park Service rangers. Rangers attempted to cite the Yukon man for running unpermitted tours in the park, and the ranger was struck in the eye when the man refused to cooperate.

Best of the Skagway Police Blotter

06/20/07: A customer asked a store clerk when she closed, and she replied 8 p.m. Then he opened his coat showing a firearm and said "I'll be back." Police were unable to locate the man.

06/20/07: Husband left home in Virginia about a month ago. Wife thinks he had a nervous breakdown and thinks he came to Alaska "because he'd always wanted to." He abandoned the wife and two kids in Virginia. She has received a couple of letters from him postmarked Skagway, and she thinks the last one, written on the 12th, sounded like a suicide letter. She thinks he's been here about two weeks and does not think he is working. Police checked around town and were unable to find him.

06/23/07: Officers extinguished smoldering rags in the back of a truck.

06/27/07: A local man called police to report a robbery – he was missing a $5 bundle of sticks from an unmanned firewood stand he had set up on Dyea Road. He had assumed the honor system would work. He started with four bundles. Two were taken and $5 each was left for them. A third was taken and only $3 was left. The fourth was taken with no money left.

06/30/07: A 40-year-old Skagway man was arrested for DUI after he was found sitting in his vehicle on private property behind a no trespassing sign at 3 a.m. After failing a set of field sobriety tests he was transported to the office and charged after he provided a breath sample indicating a .157 BAC.

FINAL RINSE – Skagway Air Service's final flight on June 30, 2007 arrived with full honors from the Skagway Volunteer Fire Department. Piper Cherokee 698 was flown by Skagway Air's vice president, Mike O'Daniel, who announced earlier in the month that the local airline was going out of business after 43 years. Company president Benny Lingle started the family-owned air charter service in 1962, and his first plane was a 1940 Stetson. The airline grew into a scheduled carrier and the decision was made to stop operating while they were "still on top." Other airlines picked up the slack, and there are still a few of the SAS planes around Southeast with the tell-tale can-can girl on the tail painted by Bea Lingle. – *Casey Dean*

2007

07/01/07: Police and fire responded to Dyea for a man who had collapsed. Co-workers on the scene had started CPR, and police applied an AED prior to ambulance transport. The 60-year-old Skagway man was pronounced dead at the clinic.

07/07/07: Police and EMS contacted the loser of a bar fight. He was transported to the clinic to get stitches, however nobody wanted to press charges.

07/07/07: Officer responded to a single vehicle rollover on Dyea Road. Investigation found that the heavily damaged unoccupied 1976 Toyota Land Cruiser had been taken by a 21-year-old man without permission from his out-of-town aunt, who asked that theft charges not be brought.

07/08/07: A 19th Avenue resident woke up to find a strange man sleeping in her house. She chased him away. Police discovered he had crashed his bike the night before while heavily intoxicated, and disoriented, walked into the similar house next door to where he belonged. Victim declined to press charges.

07/11/07: Officers and EMS personnel responded to a motor vehicle vs. pedestrian accident, where a woman walked into a bus on Second Avenue, injuring her leg.

07/13/07: Hikers advised they found a man lying under a sheet of clear plastic off the Dewey Lakes Trail. They were afraid to approach him. Police were unable to locate the man.

07/13/07: A 17-year-old Whitehorse youth was charged with minor consuming alcohol and driving after drinking, and a second friend was charged with minor consuming after police stopped the vehicle they were in for negligent driving. Both were turned over to their vacationing parents after being cited.

07/14/07: Officers responded to a complaint of noise and someone tearing up their trailer at an RV park. Officers talked to individual and advised him to keep the noise down and pick up the items he threw out of his trailer

07/16/07: A man was found sleeping in a flower bed. Due to his level of intoxication, he was brought to the police department to sleep it off.

07/17/07: A woman reported her wallet lost. The contents of the wallet were found later, but the wallet itself remained missing.

Best of the Skagway Police Blotter

07/18/07: An 83-year-old woman was reported missing by her family. She was about four hours overdue in meeting her family at the ship. She was found later when she disembarked from the train.

07/18/07: Officers responded to a report of a fight downtown. There were no charges, as the only person injured was the aggressor and he was highly intoxicated and combative. He was treated for minor injuries at the clinic and released.

07/21/07: A Dyea Road resident called and reported that a bear had been in his arctic entry earlier in the morning. Another reported a large black bear in their garden. A third was reported in a bed and breakfast Dumpster.

07/26/07: A bear was reported near the Klondike Highway where the officer used a cracker round to scare the bear away. Another bear was reported nearby where the officer used the siren to scare the bear away. A third bear was reported near the highway but it didn't stick around for the officer. This bear then came back again and again, but never stuck around after police were called.

07/28/07: Officers on patrol found a Chevy Blazer stopped in the middle of the road. The driver said that he had too many people in the vehicle, and police found five intoxicated juveniles inside, and a 21-year-old who admitted to furnishing the alcohol. The adult was charged and released, the juveniles cited and turned over to parents, and the non-drinking driver was released with a warning and a notification to his parents about being out past curfew.

07/30/07: A bear was reported in Liarsville. An officer was unable to find it, however he did warn residents about improper garbage disposal. A bear was reported in a shed just down the road, and the officer was able to haze it with a rubber round. Later an officer shot at two bears in a Dumpster. He missed the bears but did manage to take out a nearby office window.

08/02/07: Dispatch received a 911 call that a man was down and had a slow pulse at the ore terminal near the gate. Police and EMS arrived to find a man in cardiac arrest with CPR being performed. The 57-year-old Wasilla man was transported to the clinic where he was ultimately pronounced dead.

08/05/07: A man reported there was an unknown person sitting in his parked vehicle. Officers responded and found an intoxicated 24-year-old male inside whom they took home.

08/06/07: Officers responded to a 1 a.m. 911 call of a loud party going on inside an RV park bathroom. Three women inside were found yelling, and refused to quiet down, nor leave the premises when asked. Police then tried to arrest one, when they were accosted by another. Two 23-year-olds were arrested for disorderly conduct and transported to the office where they were processed and released.

08/08/07: Officers responded to a report of someone screaming near Long Bay. They contacted a group of women, who had discovered just how extremely cold the water was after they had decided to take a swim. They told officers that they would keep the screaming to a minimum as they warmed up.

08/08/07: Police conducted a death investigation aboard the Norwegian Star. The 52-year-old woman from Texas appeared to have died from natural causes.

08/09/07: Two teens, age 16 and 18, who were supposed to be on a cruise ship with their parents were reported missing. The ship was ready to depart. The parents were given an option of leaving the ship or departing without them, when the teens were located getting off the ferry from Haines.

08/14/07: A woman called and expressed concern about her son, who is working in town this summer. She had been talking to him on the phone, was disconnected, and she had been trying to reach him again with no luck. Police located the young man, whose cell phone battery had died. His mother was contacted and advised.

08/14/07: A porcupine was found inside a bar. He was "86'd" by an officer with help from patrons. This is the same porcupine that left quills in two dogs in town on 8/11. He was identified by his lack of quills when confronted.

Sgt. Ken Cox corners the porcupine, seen here perched on a table in the back of Moe's Frontier Bar, before throwing a blanket over it. This incident occurred about a month before the legendary Skagway establishment closed its doors forever. Those walls could tell some stories...and many of them were true. – *Dylan Healy*

Best of the Skagway Police Blotter

08/15/07: A man reported a black case containing four unfinished fossil walrus ivory sculptures he had been working on worth $15,000 had been taken from his vehicle while parked at the grocery store. Officers checked around town and with the cruise ships in port, however were unable to locate the case. On August 22 the victim reported that someone had taken the case and contents and dropped it off at AP&T. Nothing was missing inside.

08/16/07: Officers responded to a disturbance at the Westmark where a 45-year-old South Dakota man was fighting with hotel management. He claimed that he owned the hotel buildings and that he had purchased it with gold back when he was 15 or 16 years old. His attitude toward the officers was respectable and cooperative, and he agreed to stop yelling at the manager. An officer also unloaded a semi-automatic 9 mm pistol he had in his possession, and told him to safely pack it away during his visit.

08/18/07: After receiving complaints from several establishments that an underage minor was attempting to buy beer, police located the 19-year-old in employee housing. He supplied a breath sample indicating a BAC of .046, and was cited and released.

08/19/07: A 36-year-old Skagway woman was arrested for DUI after police found her vehicle off the roadway and high-centered near the summit. She was contacted at the U.S. border station where she had gotten a ride to after the accident. At the police station she supplied a breath sample indicating a BAC of .244, and she was cited and released.

08/21/07: A woman reported that her 86-year-old husband was missing. She was shopping and he did not want to shop. She left him sitting on a bench on Broadway Street while she shopped. When she returned he was gone. He was located on the bench in front of AB Hall where he had been sitting for two hours or more. His wife was mistaken about the location of the bench she had left him on.

08/23/07: A woman reported to police that she was punched in the stomach by her husband as they walked down Main Street toward a tavern. The intoxicated 32-year-old Skagway man was arrested for domestic violence assault.

08/25/07: A 23-year-old Skagway woman received a bloody mouth and bruised ribs after being involved in a bar fight. Due to the extreme intoxication of all involved, police separated the parties and told them the investigation would continue after they sobered up.

08/26/07: A 40-year-old Concrete, WA man was removed from a single vehicle rollover accident off Dyea Road and transported to the clinic. A blood test at the clinic showed a BAC of .326, and after treatment he was arrested for felony DUI and driving with a revoked license.

08/30/07: A crew member reportedly was caught on surveillance tape stealing an envelope with $50 in it from a desk in the recreation center office.

09/07/07: A bear was reportedly one to three miles south of the summit chasing Klondike Road Relay runners on the road. Police were unable to locate the bear.

09/07/07: A group of people in an upstairs apartment downtown were seen throwing water balloons and bottles, and also "mooning" the road relay runners. The landlord was contacted and took care of the issue.

09/10/07: Police and EMS responded to a single vehicle accident off Dyea Road, located an unoccupied van that was over a 12-foot cliff and apparently rolled at least twice. After searching the area, they were unable to locate a driver or passengers. The badly beat up driver was later found at his residence. After he was treated at the clinic, charges of driving without a license, leaving the scene of an accident, no insurance, and negligent driving were filed against the man.

09/10/07: A 59-year-old Skagway woman was issued a summons to appear on a charge of theft after an officer watched a security video showing the jewelry store employee take a tourist's camera off the store counter top and place it in her bag.

09/15/07: A man reported his $600 laptop computer stolen from his tent in an RV park. He suspects a local 16-year-old, one of three people who knew where the computer was.

09/17/07: Police received several reports of a bear near the liquor store on Second, the Westmark Hotel on Fourth, near City Hall on Seventh, and finally crossing the airport runway and the Skagway River near Ninth Avenue.

09/22/07: EMS and Rescue was dispatched to a single vehicle roll over accident with a trapped person inside on the road leading to the Dyea tidal flats. Upon arrival a responding officer found a 45-year-old Skagway man standing outside the vehicle. He refused medical attention stating the only injury he had was a small cut on one of his fingers. He was given field sobriety tests, arrested, and transported to the police station where he blew a .171 BAC. He was cited and released.

Best of the Skagway Police Blotter

09/26/07: Police were called to the U.S. Border Station where officers had detained a 32-year-old Carcross man for suspicion of driving while under the influence. The man performed a set of field sobriety tests for the SPD officer, which he failed. He was placed under arrest, transported to the police station, where he submitted to a test of his breath resulting in a .205 BAC. He was cited and released.

09/28/07: Police presence was requested by a private security firm who had chartered a plane to move jewelry from of some of the jewelry stores out of town. The firm anticipated $40 to $50 million dollars worth of property would be moved.

09/30/07: Police received word that someone has apparently set up a semi-permanent camp with teepee, fire ring and a toilet near Smuggler's Cove. Witness said there is about 20 feet of barbed wire spread out around the site.

10/11/07: A motor vehicle accident involving three vehicles was reported on Main Street. The driver of first vehicle had swerved to avoid a dog and hit two parked vehicles. No injuries to people or dog. The parked vehicles were unoccupied.

10/15/07: A $600 laptop computer was reported stolen from a store. A suspect vehicle was stopped by Canadian Customs on the way out of the country, however no laptop was found.

10/15-11/30/07: Police responded to a dozen calls of bears on porches, in alleys, in yards, walking down the street, eating garbage, and being a scary nuisance.

12/01/07: A Dyea Road man called to report he heard six shots fired and believed the grizzly bear was back. A responding officer found a neighbor had shot the bear after it had grabbed a freezer off a porch with its teeth and dragged it out onto the driveway.

12/01/07: A Skagway man was reported as unconscious and unresponsive by his wife. Responding officers arrived and found him lying on his back, not breathing with no detectable pulse. CPR was started until EMS personnel arrived and took over CPR, inserted an airway and shocked the patient three times. He was transported to the clinic where he was pronounced dead.

12/31/07: The chief was on a ferry when he called dispatch and ran a fellow passenger, who turned out had an active warrant for his arrest out of Ketchikan. As Sitka was the next stop they were advised, and the man was arrested in Sitka on the warrant by the Sitka P.D.

2008

Breaking and entering by wind and other usual suspects, vandals caught leaving their marks, lost trail walkers, unfounded reports of naked sunbathers, and more bears on the prowl.

01/12/08: Police received a complaint of theft of firewood from a residential woodpile near Second and State Street. A suspect was identified and told to repay the victim.

01/27/08: Police investigated whether someone had been inside a bed and breakfast that had been closed for the winter.

01/29/08: Police responded to a door reportedly kicked in to a business. It was determined that a door had been blown open and broken by the wind. No break-in had occurred.

02/18/08: A report was received about some broken windows on RVs in an RV park. An officer investigated the following morning and it was determined to have happened some time ago due to the lack of prints in the snow.

03/16/08: A man reported that sometime overnight someone entered his home and stole a laptop computer and a wallet. Police identified a neighboring juvenile suspect and the property was recovered.

03/20/08: EMTs responded via helicopter and rescue boat to the Kasidaya Creek hydroelectric facility for the report of an industrial accident which resulted in a fatality.

03/24/08: A vacant home was reported entered and ransacked, however nothing appeared missing. Two local juvenile suspects were identified and referred.

Best of the Skagway Police Blotter

03/25/08: A Washington woman was arrested on a felony warrant for escaping from community custody in that state and returned to jail.

04/04/08: A chair was discovered under a broken window to another vacant residence. The same juvenile suspects from the week before confessed to being responsible. No entry was gained to this residence.

SAFETY FIRST – Public Works crew foreman Grant Lawson and Tyson Ames paint yellow warning stripes on the boardwalk by the NPS Visitor Center on Broadway in advance of the 2008 summer season.

04/06/08: Police responded to a report of a person refusing to leave the Pizza Station. Individual was removed by officers, who refused to leave until they arrived because he felt disrespected by the bartender. The bar asked to press trespass charges.

04/15/08: A 37-year-old Skagway man was arrested for domestic violence assault for reported physical abuse to his girlfriend inside their residence.

04/22/08: Report of a suspicious person who showed up at a house at 6:30 this morning inquiring why people were living on his property. Officers had the same problem last year, when he claimed to have bought the Westmark Hotel with gold when he was 15-years-old.

04/23/08: A rock face was reported spray-painted at Yakutania Point. Local subjects were identified when the responding officer recognized several of the first names inside a painted heart.

05/03/08: Police took a report of a hit and run traffic collision involving a city pump house on Alaska Street. The suspect driver fessed up at the station two days later, advising she knew officers were searching for her.

05/06/08: An intoxicated subject had entered a residence on 11th Avenue and had passed out on a couch. Officers removed him and took him home.

2008

05/15/08: Officers responded to Liarsville and used non-lethal rubber bullets to haze a nuisance black bear out of the area.

05/15/08: Officers responded to a report of a loud party in employee housing at Third and State. A small amount of marijuana was confiscated and destroyed. Four people in the group were cited for underage drinking.

05/16/08: A complaint was received of a person soliciting tours near the Railroad Dock. After further investigation and interviews, the individual was cited for off premises canvassing and prohibited solicitation.

05/19/08: Police responded to the clinic to help with a combative injured man who may have been in a fight. Investigation revealed that he had been driving – without permission or a valid driver's license – a company van which he crashed near Liarsville while under the influence of intoxicants. Turned out the beer he had been drinking was stolen from the company bar. After supplying a breath sample indicating .19 BAC, the 27-year-old Skagway man was charged with DUI and burglary.

05/21/08: A 911 call was received about a man following another man around with a gun. An officer responded to the area and contacted two men who recently opened a new business in town. A 20-gauge shotgun and a knife were taken from them, and they were told they could retrieve them when they had worked out their argument.

05/23/08: A report was received about a dog that had possibly been abandoned and tied up behind the bank. The dog was brought to the pound. The owner of the dog came by within a half hour and retrieved the dog. It had not been abandoned.

05/25/08: Officers pulled over a vehicle, steaming from heavy front-end damage on Dyea Road. A Dyea resident, 51, was arrested on a DUI charge. Officers located a vehicle she had struck and damaged on 10th before fleeing the scene. After suppling a breath sample indicating a .22 BAC, she was cited and driven home.

05/25/08: A citation for minor consuming alcohol was issued to a 20-year-old man whom police contacted near Pullen Pond. Two hours later police received a report of a man who matched the description wandering into a Main Street residence appearing "intoxicated and confused." The man did not belong to that residence, and left before police arrival.

Best of the Skagway Police Blotter

05/29/08: A report was received of possible bear baiting on the Dyea Road near the overlook.

06/01/08: Officers found a 45-year-old man, who was obviously intoxicated, sitting behind the wheel of his pickup near Main Street and decided to give him a ride to his Dyea residence to keep him from driving. Later in the shift, they noticed the man driving the truck from town toward Dyea Road. The man told the officers he had ridden his bicycle back into town to retrieve the truck. The man was arrested for DUI and taken to the station where he blew a .15 BAC. He was cited and held until he sobered up.

06/06/08: An intoxicated man was given a ride home by officers after he was found lying in an alley. He had crashed his bicycle into some bushes.

06/06/08: Officers responded to a complaint of an intoxicated foul-mouthed person in the downtown area. It turned out that the caller was the intoxicated foul-mouthed person. She was given a ride home.

06/07/08: A 27-year-old seasonal resident from Washington, was arrested on a warrant for failure to appear for arraignment on a May 19 DUI charge. Bail was posted and subject was released.

06/07/08: A report was received of someone stealing milk cartons from the grocery store. Officers responded but were unable to locate any one in the area or around town matching the description given.

06/09/08: A business reported that a former employee stole a company laptop computer and a company credit card. The employee was located through credit card purchases and was arrested by Port of Seattle Police at the Seattle airport.

06/10/08: A report was received of an intoxicated man entering a home where he did not belong. Officers responded and took the man to his home.

06/11/08: An officer investigated a report of a dog bite. The owner of the dog was located and licensed the dog. The dog was quarantined at the owner's residence for five days.

06/11/08: Officers responded to a noise complaint and found two people arguing very loudly over an unpaid debt. The debt was paid and they agreed to stop yelling.

06/12/08: An officer responded to a report of a naked sunbather near the Captain William Moore suspension bridge. No sunbathers were located, naked or clothed.

06/12/08: Officers responded to a loud party complaint at an RV park. Two citations were issued for minor consuming alcohol.

06/13/08: A 27-year-old Skagway resident was arrested for driving under the influence of alcohol after police noticed her driving aimlessly through town, failing to signal at each turn. She was cited and released after agreeing to supply a breath sample indicating a BAC of .17.

06/13/08: "Tecumseh," a Native American sculpture made of wood usually found in front of a Broadway Street business, was reported hanging from the Kirmse's "clock" on the cliffs above town, along with a bicycle. The owner of "Tecumseh" was contacted. It is unknown how "Tecumseh" got up to the clock.

06/14/08: A Skagway man, 25, was arrested for felony third degree assault for threatening people with a knife inside employee housing. He was transported to Lemon Creek Correctional Center in Juneau while awaiting trial.

06/14/08: Two citations for minor consuming alcohol were issued to underage people caught inside the beer garden at the Solstice Party. Both were transported home and turned over to adults.

KIDNAP VICTIM TAKES PLUNGE – Tecumseh, the cigar store sculpture who has been a fixture out front and even on top of the old Golden North Hotel for the past few years, was kidnapped for a third time around June 10. He turned up on Friday the 13th as a hand on the "Kirmse's Clock" on the east hillside. The wooden statue was hung from a rope, appearing as a minute hand at the 5-minute mark. Owner Dennis Corrington said he wrote up a missing person's report a couple days earlier when the statue went missing from its shackles on the boardwalk outside his gift shop:

MISSING: Native American male, 5'6", about 120 pounds, silent, doesn't smile, cracked facial features from being in the sun a lot, has quit smoking but still carries cigars just in case he wants to have one, as a temptation.

Corrington said Tecumseh had been kidnapped twice before – in 2004 and 2006 – so he then put it on top of the hotel. When the Historic District Commission questioned the move, Corrington told them it was just two feet west of where it was permitted to be. "It said nothing about height." He brought it down this summer to place outside the gift shop, and it lasted about a month before being kidnapped again. "I figure they had to be male, more than one, probably climbers, and alcohol was involved. Maybe they used a 4-wheeler to get it up the access road and then hoist it up there," he said. The statue was first spotted on the 13th – someone even thought it was a real body (see blotter). But it disappeared again on June 18. Tecumseh may have met his final demise. "The word I got back was it was at the bottom of the rock pile," Corrington said. "The knot was untied, or maybe it was a suicide dive?" – *JB*

Best of the Skagway Police Blotter

06/15/08: Police investigated a burglary at the clinic where suspects entered through an unsecured window and took approximately $300 from a cash box. Also, at the neighboring tribal council office, a screen was found cut on two windows. An 18-year-old seasonal worker was later arrested and charged.

06/18/08: A burglary was reported at an unlocked trailer residence inside an RV park. The trailer was ransacked. Stolen items worth an estimated $1,000 include an MP3 player, an iPod and charger, two cameras, and some memory cards.

06/20/08: Officers were dispatched to a fight in progress between two women. Police found one lying on the roadway with a bloody nose, but she declined to press charges against the other. Alcohol was a significant factor.

06/24/08: A man reported being assaulted by his boss. The case was turned over to the District Attorney's office for review. All persons involved have since left town.

06/24/08: A man called dispatch from his cell phone asking for directions to his ship from the Dewey Lakes Trail. He was able to get back to his ship before it left port.

06/26/08: Almost $80,000 was reported stolen from a company safe. The assaultive boss in an earlier call was determined to be the lead suspect, however he unexpectedly left town during the investigation. Police had him searched at a Washington border crossing where he had $8,000 in cash and numerous articles of company clothing still with the sales tags intact. In August the man was contacted in Seattle leaving a cruise ship that had visited Skagway. He had over 50,000 undeclared dollars on him this time.

06/29/08: A large store on Broadway reported it had been burglarized to the tune of almost $132,000, even though $600 in cash in plain sight was left behind. Entry was gained by a roof window. Police gained a confession from a store shipping clerk, who was also a suspect in the earlier clinic break-in.

07/02/08: Search and Rescue teams were dispatched for an overdue hiker somewhere on the Dewey Lakes Trail. He had gotten off trail and was lost according to reports from his parents, who had spoken to him on his cell phone. Contact via cell by searchers was established but due to a low battery his phone battery died during the search. He was finally located six hours after initial response by SAR.

07/07/08: A man called 911 to report getting bad food in a local restaurant. He was not going to pay for the food and wanted us to know in case the restaurant called.

2008

07/14/08: Two men were contacted by SPD and advised they cannot play Frisbee on the airport tarmac.

07/14/08: A bench was reported missing from in front of a jewelry store. The store reported a week earlier that a bench had been thrown into the street, breaking it.

07/15/08: Police investigated a person suspected of operating a boat charter without the proper licenses.

07/19/08: Police contacted a man in a motel room yelling obscenities. He told officers he was upset he couldn't find something in his luggage. The next day police were called when he refused to pay his bar bill. After paying, he was told he was no longer welcome on the property.

07/23/08: Police and EMS responded to the visitor center to aid people who had bear spray in their eyes.

07/24/08: Police contacted bar management, concerned that the building was too crowded and over occupancy limit. The bar owner told police she didn't think there was a limit due to number of exits available. The state fire marshal issued new occupancy signs to be mounted.

08/02/08: Police were advised of a momma bear and three cubs visiting the salmon bake in Liarsville. Bears were heading off on officer's arrival. Bears continued to visit Dumpsters around town for a couple of weeks before disappearing.

08/09/08: Police and SAR responded to assist a raft full of boaters trapped against a piling under the Skagway River bridge.

PRESSED INTO SERVICE – Onlookers gather as Search and Rescue's Dan Fangmeier unties a raft pinned against the pilings of the Pat Moore footbridge. When SAR arrived at the scene, four of the five rafters had made it to shore. The fifth swam to shore after their arrival. – *Ken Cox, SPD*

Best of the Skagway Police Blotter

08/10/08: An intoxicated Whitehorse man was held for the night after he was found downtown unable to remember who he was or where he was.

08/16/08: Two women were contacted at Mollie Walsh Park. Officers determined that they had played on a piece of equipment intended for small children and had broken it.

08/19/08: A man called 911 to complain that a local store would not refund him on a purchase. He had found the same item for a lot less at another store.

08/19/08: A woman called 911 and reported a dog had been hit by a car. Officers determined the dog had not been hit; rather it was just old and walked slowly with a limp.

08/23/08: A woman reported her van stolen or towed. The vehicle was located parked in a different location that she thought she had parked.

08/25/08: A man reported his wallet containing approximately $400 was stolen from the locker room at the recreation center. A juvenile suspect was identified and he and his parents agreed to make restitution.

08/26/08: An officer was dispatched to a downtown jewelry store to investigate a broken window. A rock was found inside the store but there was nothing taken and entry had not been made by the rock thrower.

08/27/08: Two passports were found in the men's rest room at a local bar. The two female owners of the passports were on a ship that had already departed.

08/28/08: A camper was found at Pullen Pond in front of the "No Camping" sign. He moved on.

08/30/08: A 44-year-old visitor from Quebec was arrested for driving under the influence of alcohol after police observed him failing to stop for a stop sign. He agreed to provide police with a blood sample indicating a .89 BAC and was cited and released on a $5,000 secured bond.

09/01/08: A counterfeit $100 bill was confiscated from a man from Mexico who tried to spend it at a local store. He claimed to have received it from a bank in Mexico City.

2008

09/03/08: Two reports of bears getting into Dumpsters were taken. The Dumpster-diving bears were chased off both times by noise.

09/04/08: A man reported losing his wallet. He insisted that he was the victim of a pocket picker. He called later and advised that his wallet had been left aboard his ship, safe and sound in his cabin.

09/10/08: A local tour operator reported that he had run over a man's foot with his van. The man refused any help, stated he was in a hurry to get back to his ship and left the area.

09/13/08: A report of a man walking into a van was received. He was located and uninjured; the van suffered minor damage.

09/15/08: Police received a complaint of a driver pitching a liquor bottle out of a badly weaving vehicle on Main Street. Officers located the vehicle parked in a loading zone near the liquor store. A 67-year-old Florida visitor was arrested for DUI. He provided a breath sample indicating a .15 BAC and was cited and released.

09/18/08: A woman reported that her parked vehicle had been hit by a bus. After an investigation, the driver of the bus was issued a citation for unsafe backing.

09/18/08: A 43-year-old Skagway woman was arrested for DUI after police watched her make several driving mistakes. She agreed to provide police with a blood sample indicating a .19 BAC and was cited and released on a $1,000 cash only bail, due to a prior DUI conviction.

09/19/08: A man reported that his pants and wallet had been stolen from his room. An officer responded and checked his room. The pants and wallet were located under his mattress.

09/24/08: An officer was dispatched to a store downtown for a report of counterfeit cash. The cash in question was determined to be genuine. It was just old.

09/29/08: A boat and trailer was dumped in West Creek about a half mile past the second bridge up the road. It looked like it had been backed in and abandoned. It had coolers, gas cans, and dolphin boat fenders in it. Boat was pulled out by Public Works and moved to storage. Police still trying to determine ownership.

Best of the Skagway Police Blotter

10/03/08: A woman called and reported that a bag of groceries was stolen from her car.

10/23/08: Police received a complaint of a mother bear and three cubs in a yard on 19th Avenue. An officer responded and found all four bears up trees inside the fenced yard. Rubber rounds convinced the mother to leave, but only convinced the cubs to leave one tree and climb another.

10/27/08: An officer assisted a group of people who had locked their keys in their vehicle at the summit.

10/27/08: A 20-year-old seasonal resident was arrested for theft of police equipment. A police flashlight had been left in his apartment during an earlier call, and he had denied having it later when asked. The flashlight was found in his possession when police returned on still another call to the residence.

11/12/08: A bear reportedly knocked over a residential heating fuel tank, causing a small spill.

12/09/08: A winter caretaker called police after footprints in the snow led into a building he was watching. Police found footprints throughout the building, but not who made them. The caretaker found nothing missing, and thought he had the only set of keys to the building.

12/10/08: A man reported that he had been threatened by someone named "Wade" who had called his cell. The man said "Wade" wanted him to come down to the Pizza Station and face him like a man, and if he didn't, he'd find him tomorrow. The man stated he did not know anyone named "Wade," or why he would want to fight him. Police then met the alleged "Wade" at the Station, who admitted calling the man, but was too intoxicated to talk further. He agreed to come in to SPD in the morning after he sobered up. He did not show up as promised, and when police identified him, they discovered he was on probation out of Fairbanks and supposed to be abstaining from alcohol. "Wade" was located, arrested and turned over to troopers for a probation violation.

12/19/08: Police stopped a 50-year-old Ninth Avenue resident for failing to stop at a stop sign and also found two glass pipes with trace amounts of methamphetamine and a bottle of assorted prescription pills.

12/21/08: Trees, power lines, a stop sign, and a canoe were all reported flying in high winds. Several doors were reportedly blown open as well.

Heard on the Wind

More puzzling questions posed by Skagway's visitors

A couple gets off the Sun Princess and tells a ship photographer: "We don't want our picture taken – we look like tourists." – 05/30/03

A guide on a kayak tour of the lakes around Fraser, B.C. informed his group that the gold fields were another 500 miles inland from where they were paddling. One client gazed at the mountains in the distance and asked, "Can we see them from here?" – 06/27/03

A man with his girlfriend at the Railroad Dock asked what was the elevation, and was told it was sea level.

"Sea level?" was the curious query.

"That is the sea and we are at sea level," he was again told. The Skagwayan kept hoping the man wouldn't further prove his stupidity in front of his girlfriend.

"How high does it get?" he asked. – 06/27/03

A woman asked someone in the hardware store, "How many feet below sea level are we?"

The reply was that we're a few feet above sea level, to which she responded, "I don't think so, I saw the dikes holding back the sea when we came in on the ship!" - 08/29/03

A local 13-year-old, on meeting the new exchange student from Germany, asked, "Do you speak German?" – 08/29/03

Two women visitors met up on the boardwalk and this is their exchange: "What did you see on the tour?" one asks. "Trees, trees, rocks, rocks, trees, trees, rocks, rocks," is her reply. – 08/23/03

"This is not what it was like in the brochure – it was sunny in the brochure." – 09/12/03

HEARD ON THE WIND

"If this is a rainforest, where are all the parrots and monkeys?" – 09/12/03

A "Big White" movie actor, who has played everything from a Boston bartender on TV to a "Natural Born Killer," was advised to take some sunscreen up to the pass for his day of filming on the white snow in the bright sun.
He refused.
"I'm from Malibu, man," he reportedly said. "I don't burn."
Upon his return, this California boy was "Panama Red" and hurting. – 05/14/03

Overheard going into an expresso bar, "This is the nicest little town we've been to, except for Anchorage. That was beautiful." – 05/14/04

As two of the Days of '98 Show girls hung out the windows of the Eagles Hall, a female passerby asked Soapy Smith, "Do you really have whores up there?"
Soapy's response: "Are you looking for work?" – 05/28/04

A visitor got off the cruise ship, looked up, admired the mountains around Skagway, and said, "It is so beautiful here, but it is such a shame they clear-cut the tops off all these mountains!" – 06/11/04

And someone who knows more than we do: "Just imagine, they created these little towns just for the cruise ships." – 06/25/04

After a newsie pointed out seals in the water by the Broadway Dock, a visitor asked, "When will they be back? We have to go on our tour now." – 08/13/04

A man on a smoke break asked a reporter, "What town are we in? All these towns look the same to me." – 08/13/04

A bike tour operator on a summit tour was asked, "Do we ride down the glacier?" – 08/27/04

A woman got her husband's attention, pointed to the tops of the mountains down the inlet and said, "Oh, look at those glaciers up there – were they there this morning?" – 08/27/04

Said by a tourist while on a Chilkoot hike and float tour, "Where do you put the glacial silt when all us tourists go away?" – 08/27/04

HEARD ON THE WIND

A cruise passenger stopped to admire the beautiful ice sculpture on a ship and then asked a member of the wait staff, "What is that made of?"

"Ice."

"What's the ice made of?" – 08/27/04

And back on the ship, a visitor asked someone at the shore excursion desk if the elevator went to the front of the ship, but that didn't top this one: "What time will it be at this time tomorrow?" – 08/27/04

"The northern lights are reflections of the glaciers, right?" – 09/24/04

"At what elevation do sheep become mountain goats?" – 09/24/04

After a train guide informed passengers about the continental divide, and how water from Summit Lake flows toward the Yukon, and water on the U.S. side flows down to the ocean, a visitor asked, "How does the water know which way to go?" – 05/13/05

Down on the Broadway Dock one morning, a man gestured to the water and asked, "So, does that lake ever freeze up?" – 06/10/05

A visitor looking at the pollen on the water asked, "Is that gold dust?" – 06/24/05

A tourist asks a clerk, "Can I trade in the shoes I'm wearing that I bought in Juneau for a smaller size here in Skagway at your store?" – 07/08/05

STIPKA ON THE STICK – In 2002, Skagway Visitor Center employee Ben Pickett (center) presented Maria Stipka (left) with $20 for coming closest to correctly guessing the number of sticks on A.B. Hall. Pickett said he counted the pieces of driftwood on his breaks for a week, coming up with a total of 8,833. Tourism Director Buckwheat Donahue (right) and the VC staff then collected more than 200 guesses over two days. Stipka, a waitperson at the Bonanza, guessed 9,099. "Nine is my lucky number," she said. Next closest were Doreen Cooper with 9,134 and Ralf Gorichanaz with 8,450. Guesses ranged from 1,000 to 40,000, Pickett said. The sticks were first applied to the false front by artist Charlie Walker about 100 years ago, and it was rumored there were about 10,000 pieces. Thanks to the CVB staff, we now know the true total.

HEARD ON THE WIND

Downtown one day, a woman was heard telling her husband, "You know, that woman we met, she's a Native Alaskan. She was born in the Yukon!" – 07/22/05

A customer walks into the bookstore and notices the "Cell Phone Free Zone" sign, then turns to her husband and says, "Look honey, you can use your cell phone for free in here." – 07/22/05

A man dressed in chain store polyester asked for a bag for his newspaper, with this excuse: "I don't mind people knowing I'm a tourist, but I don't want them to think I'm a rich tourist carrying the Wall Street Journal." – 08/12/05

Upon hearing of the decline of Skagway's population after the gold rush, a woman on a town tour remarked, "It's a good thing the jewelry stores came in and saved the town." – 08/26/05

FIRST DAY TOUR GREETERS – Tour reps Jeff Neis of Skagway Street Car Co., Mark Nadeau of the Red Onion, and Megan Taft of Holland America-Princess wait for the first wave of visitors heading off the Railroad Dock at the start of the 2010 season.

At a photo gallery on a ship where hundreds of photos from the cruise are displayed, more than one visitor has remarked, "How do I know which one is me?"
– 08/26/05

A guy off the ferry pointed to the mountain peaks and asked, "What's that snow doing up there?" The same guy, while waiting for his ride to a hotel, pointed to the assembled vehicles in the parking lot and asked, "What are those cars doing here?" – 09/23/05

A visitor to a shop overheard a conversation about seeing the northern lights recently in the Yukon, and then asked the owner if there is a season for the lights. The visitor was told winter is best when there is more darkness, to which the visitor replied, "Is this winter?" – 09/23/05

2009

Strange water bodies, wolf, coyote and rogue beaver join bears in disturbing the peace, fish fondlers cited, and Broadway pile-ups investigated.

02/02/09: A man reported he had left his truck parked overnight near the Eagles and walked home after drinking. He discovered $400 worth of tools missing when he returned to retrieve the vehicle.

02/06/09: A Skagway man, 34, was stopped for speeding and subsequently arrested for DUI. After agreeing to provide a breath sample indicating a BAC of .09, he was cited and released.

03/10/09: A wolf was seen in a residential area. An officer responded and observed and followed the wolf leaving the area heading toward Lower Lake on the trail. The wolf was reported in town several more times this week.

03/11/09: An officer responded to a motor vehicle accident at approximately 10 mile Klondike Highway. A van rear-ended the DOT snow blower that was parked on the side of the highway. There was significant damage to the van but no injuries.

03/22/09: Numerous coyote sightings were reported around town over a week-long period.

03/26/09: A man came in and reported an assault that had occurred in a bar five months earlier. The victim waited so long to report it as he was trying to give the suspect, a friend, time to make the $8,000 in damages to his face right.

Best of the Skagway Police Blotter

03/29/09: A report of a body in the Taiya Inlet was received. It had been discovered by scuba divers. Police, water rescue and EMT personnel responded. Divers brought the "body" to shore and it was determined to be the carcass of a bear. State Fish and Game was contacted and they requested that the carcass be weighted down and sunk back into the inlet.

04/12/09: An officer assisted a man who was locked out of his house.

04/26/09: An officer responded to a report of a domestic dispute. There was no violence involved but the couple agreed to separate for the night.

04/26/09: Officer and EMS personnel responded to a report of an at-home death. Death was from natural causes. This was the first of three home deaths of local residents this year.

04/30/09: A caller reported an unknown man sleeping on his dining table. The intoxicated man was awakened and taken home by officers.

05/06/09: Police and Search & Rescue personnel with Serv-U (rescue boat), and a TEMSCO helicopter were dispatched to assist Haines Search and Rescue on a missing persons report. Three Haines residents had tried to canoe to Skagway in a plastic 14' Colman canoe. The capsized canoe was discovered near Lutak Inlet. Personnel assisted in the recovery of two bodies. The third man had reached the shore safely and survived.

05/10/09: Officers responded to a report of a domestic disturbance in a campground. The situation was deemed under control. Alcohol was a factor.

05/10/09: Police located a "tent city" of five illegal campsites set up on the hillside above town.

05/11/09: An officer was dispatched to investigate the report of a man lying in the middle of the highway taking pictures. The man was gone when officers arrived.

05/14/09: Intoxicated females stole a pedi-cab. The owner was able to get it back.

05/14/09: An officer observed girls set a case of beer down in the street and then go into the Red Onion. He followed them in and asked one of them about it, however she denied having had anything to do with the beer. The officer brought the abandoned property to the station where it was disposed of.

05/15/09: Numerous folks were reportedly climbing on the Recreation Center roof.

05/19/09: An elderly couple appeared at the police department seeking assistance after they were removed from a cruise ship for being disruptive.

05/25/09: An outhouse fell off of a trailer and through a residential window at 19th and Alaska Street.

05/26/09: A man complained about being yelled at by a business owner on Second Avenue for using "his" loading zone.

06/02/09: An officer assisted a person who had locked their keys in a running vehicle.

06/02/09: A police patrol bicycle collided with a photographer standing in the roadway.

06/03/09: An officer responded to a report of a motor vehicle accident. There were no injuries but significant damage was reported to a tour vehicle struck by a bus. The bus left the area without stopping, however the driver was apparently unaware of the collision.

06/04/09: Jewelry valued at $440 was reported shoplifted from a downtown shop.

06/06/09: A Skagway man was arrested for DUI. He was found passed out behind the wheel of his parked vehicle and transported to the de-

Security wasn't very tight when Governor Sarah Palin came to Skagway. Here she clutches her mocha and Blackberry as she greets baby Annabelle Eskins and mom Maria.

Governor pops into Skagway

Governor Sarah Palin made a brief visit to Skagway on April 29, 2009, her first trip back to her original Alaska home since 2007 and the first since her 2008 vice presidential run. The governor was at a scheduled visit in Haines earlier in the day to sign a bill extending benefits to 26 members of the old Alaska Territorial Guard.

A day earlier, word leaked from Haines sources that the governor would be taking the ferry LeConte over to Skagway. When she arrived, the SHS Student Council welcomed her with a sign. She then drove with Dyea friend Kathy Hosford to Glacial Smoothies, where her staff had set up a meeting with Mayor Tom Cochran and Assemblyman Mike Korsmo.

The governor posed for photos inside and outside, ordered an iced mocha, and met with the borough representatives for about 10 minutes. Before heading to the airport, the governor made a quick stop at her old Skagway home at First and Main.

She did not take questions from the media, as time was short, but she said she would answer questions submitted by e-mail through the press office.

The governor did follow through with the e-interview, but alas, this was her last visit to Skagway as governor. She resigned in July of 2009. – JB

partment, where rather than provide a breath sample he decided he was having heart problems and insisted on an ambulance to take him to the clinic. Officers obtained a warrant for a blood sample from the clinic. The man disappeared after being transported to a Juneau hospital, and a warrant was issued for his arrest for failing to appear for court.

06/08/09: An officer responded to a motor vehicle accident downtown involving two tour buses. There were no injuries and minor damages were reported on both vehicles.

06/14/09: A woman reported that her laptop computer was stolen from her vehicle. The unlocked vehicle had been left overnight next to a downtown bar and the laptop had been visible on the front seat.

GLACIER BEAR – A black bear roams the Davidson Glacier near Haines. – *Andrew Cremata*

06/16/09: A man reported that his apartment had been broken into. Three guitars and 200 movies were missing. Suspect was identified and all stolen items were retrieved. Theft was retaliation for an earlier assault.

06/16/09: A woman reported that her apartment was broken into but nothing was stolen. This was also tied to the above assault/theft case.

06/22/09: A call was received reporting that four trees were cut down near the Railroad Dock. After investigation, a beaver was named the culprit.

06/25/09: Officers responded to a report of a bear in Mountain View RV Park. The bear had gotten into a carelessly stored food container. Officers fired rubber rounds at the bear and he left the area. The bear came back later and took a loaf of bread off of a picnic table at another campsite. All the occupants were told to securely store their food. The same bear was seen later trying to get into the Dumpster behind the Borough offices and later a Dumpster at a restaurant on Congress Way.

06/26/09: A bear was seen near 18th and State. It was discovered later that it had gotten into some garbage cans and Dumpsters in the area.

06/28/09: A black bear was seen getting into garbage cans at the north end of town. He was shot twice with rubber rounds and was not seen the rest of the night.

06/29/09: A bear was seen on the railroad tracks near Fifth Avenue. It was scared off by noise from the train. He was seen later near 10th Avenue and a rubber round was shot at him. He left the area and headed across town toward the river.

06/30/09: A life size wooden Native American ("Tecumseh" again) was seen standing on the south end of Broadway Street near the access road to the harbor. His owner was contacted, and he has found his way back to his usual perch by the Golden North Hotel.

06/30/09: A bear was seen trying to get into garbage near Sixth and State Street. An officer followed him south and the bear eventually headed up the hillside.

07/01/09: A bear was reported in a Dumpster near Sixth and Broadway. Later in the day a bear was seen near the Borough offices between Mollie Walsh Park and the railroad tracks. An officer hit the bear with a rubber bullet and it ran up the hillside.

07/02/09: A bear was seen in the area of Fifth and Alaska. An officer responded but the bear was gone when he arrived. A bear was later reported near Fifth and Spring but had also disappeared.

07/05/09: A bear was seen getting into garbage near 22nd and Main Street. An officer fired a cracker round at the bear and sent it up the hillside.

07/05/09: An officer investigated a report of a vehicular hit and run accident in the small boat harbor parking lot. Car suffered a serious dent to the driver's door.

07/08/09: A black bear was seen near Second and Spring downtown. He later went into the woods. A black bear was seen in a campground just north of downtown. He later got into the Dumpster at the campground. Eventually an officer was able to chase the bear off. An officer responded to a report of a

Best of the Skagway Police Blotter

bear in a Dyea Road residence. The bear went in through a small window. There was minimal damage but the bear did leave a mess in the kitchen. The bear was chased off by noise made by the occupants.

07/09/09: Officers responded to a report of a bear in a residence. The bear was still inside when officers arrived and escaped out the same window he had entered through. Officers hazed it with a couple of impact rounds. The bear came back to the residence later in the evening but did not enter the home. The owner is planning on shooting the bear should it return.

07/09/09: A homeless person is suspected of putting a small rock in a doorjamb and sleeping in the Eagles Hall at night.

07/11/09: Officers responded to a report of a bear getting into a freezer at a restaurant. The officers determined that the bear was the same bear that has been a problem all around town. The bear was shot and killed by police.

07/11/09: Police were asked to remove a 29-year-old Skagway man who refused to leave a bar. The next day they delivered a letter to him from the owners barring him from reentry.

07/12/09: Police, EMS and Fire personnel were dispatched for a report of a vehicle rollover at approximately 5 Mile Klondike Highway. Upon arrival it was discovered that no one had been injured. The accident was caused by the driver panicking when a bee flew into the vehicle and up his shirt.

07/16/09: A pedestrian walked into the side of a passing vehicle on Broadway Street, breaking the bone in the small finger of his left hand.

07/16/09: Police were asked to investigate the death of an elderly Minnesota man aboard a cruise ship. Visitor apparently died of natural causes.

07/18/09: Police refereed a shouting match at the grocery store between a customer attempting to return product and management. The shopper threw a bag of expired spinach at the manager.

07/19/09: Police gained entry into a tour bus waiting to load passengers at the train depot in which the keys had been locked inside.

07/20/09: A residence under repair was broken into and tools were taken.

2009

07/20/09: An officer was dispatched to a fist fight in progress – yelling and screaming, knock down, drag out fight – at Pullen RV Park. Upon arrival the officer discovered no violence had taken place, only yelling. The couple was advised to separate for the rest of the evening.

07/23/09: A tour company manager reported they had just let an employee go for refusing a drug test. It didn't go well and he fears this person may retaliate by damaging the buses parked near Jewell Gardens on the Klondike Highway.

07/24/09: Officers responded to a domestic dispute. The couple agreed to separate for the night. Mass consumption of alcohol was a factor.

07/28/09: A store clerk noticed a $200 kaleidoscope was missing and apparently shoplifted.

07/31/09: Police contacted a large party at employee housing on State Street, once over the size of the bonfire and once over excessive noise. Later police responded to the clinic to assist with an intoxicated man who fell into the fire at the party. The fire department cancelled the burn permit for that address the next day.

08/01/09: An officer was dispatched for a report of a dead dog in the creek. Upon arrival it was discovered not to be a dog but a very waterlogged teddy bear.

08/01/09: A citation was issued to a Minnesota man for snagging salmon in Pullen Pond.

08/01/09: Officers and fire personnel responded to a report of a fire under an outside heating fuel tank at a residence. The fire was extinguished.

08/02/09: Just after midnight police noticed a man with an uneven gait get ready to drive away from a downtown bar and asked him if he would take a PBT (portable breath test). It showed .07 BAC (.08 is the legal limit) and he was asked not to drive. The gentleman was cooperative.

08/06/09: A 16-year-old California man was issued a citation for intentionally snagging salmon in Pullen Pond after being repeatedly warned not to do so.

08/06/09: Officers asked a large party from a cruise ship to leave Pullen Park for having open containers, throwing rocks at and poking fish with sticks.

Best of the Skagway Police Blotter

08/06/09: Officers responded to a complaint of an intoxicated man being obnoxious. The intoxicated obnoxious man was picked up and taken to his home.

08/07/09: Two men were contacted in a no parking zone. They had set up a camp stove and chairs and were handing out religious pamphlets. When asked to move on, they said they were exercising their constitutional rights. They were finally convinced there were no constitutional rights to parking and left for greener pastures.

08/07/09: Police assisted with an unruly ex-employee who was "yelling and breaking things."

08/09/09: Police advised two men to go sleep in the woods rather than stay home and get yelled at by a sister over an affair she thought one of them was involved in.

08/09/09: A 56-year-old Skagway man was cited for snagging salmon and fishing without a license.

08/10 to 8/13/09: Eleven people were contacted and issued warnings for grabbing fish from Pullen Pond or the creek.

08/15/09: A 24-year-old Whitehorse man was arrested for theft after an officer found him stealing diesel fuel from the DOT shops fuel tank. He was arraigned later in the day and pleaded guilty. He paid fines and restitution in the amount of $1,100. He is also a suspect for at least two other reports of missing fuel.

08/16/09: After receiving a report from a concerned citizen, police checked for warrants on a 46-year-old Seattle man. He is a convicted sex offender in Washington, with an outstanding arrest warrant for escape from community custody. He was arrested and held at the Skagway jail while awaiting transport to Lemon Creek in Juneau and from there to Washington.

08/18/09: A visitor approached dispatch and asked if we knew about the "protesting hippies" at Centennial Park. He said they are protesting global warming by shaving their heads and throwing their hair on the ground.

08/19/09: The parents of six children were contacted and issued a warning for letting the children grab fish out of Pullen Creek.

08/26/09: A ring was found on the boardwalk downtown and brought to the police department. The ring was later identified and claimed by the very relieved owner. The ring has an estimated value of $30,000.

08/26/09: A Skagway woman reported that she had been sexually assaulted by an acquaintance after a night of drinking together. Case was investigated and referred to the District Attorney for possible charges.

08/27/09: Police responded to the hostel for a disturbance revolving around whether a light should be turned on. Police settled the issue once, however on the second call officers transported one of the men to a hotel to sleep it off.

08/31/09: Police received a report that a tour bus driver had stopped next to a creek and pulled out a fish for his passengers to photograph. Tour bus driver said it was not him, but a passenger who had fondled the fish. Company manager instructed the buses to not stop by the creek.

OOPS - A Gray Line bus side-swiped its cousin, a Princess bus, as it turned onto Eighth on a rainy May 26. Proof that the Holland America-Princess merger extends to all phases of operation. – *Ray Calver*

08/31/09: A woman called and reported seeing light from flashlights in a closed business. An officer responded and found the owners in the building making repairs.

09/02/09: Police investigated the death of a crew member aboard a cruise ship. Death appeared to be from natural causes, body was shipped to the medical examiner.

09/04/09: A 49-year-old seasonal worker from Anchorage was arrested for DUI. He refused to provide a breath sample, for which he was also cited. He was released on $1,000 bail, as this was his second DUI charge.

Best of the Skagway Police Blotter

09/04/09: An 8-year-old in town for her cousin's wedding was separated from her family and unable to find her way home. She contacted a resident, who called police, who called the magistrate, who recognized the wedding party.

09/05/09: Search and Rescue personnel were dispatch to the AB Mountain trail due to a report of a flashing light thought to be a distress signal. Up the trail campers were contacted by searchers, and they were fine. They thought it would be fun to flash the police with their light.

09/13/09: A 39-year-old Skagway woman came to the department advising she was having suicidal thoughts. Police contacted the mental health provider who supplied officers with a temporary supply of medications to dole out. She was later taken into protective custody and transported to Juneau.

09/15/09: Police stood by as cruise ship security attempted to remove a 42-year-old Pennsylvania man who had reportedly "flashed" a knife at another man the night before near Glacier Bay. The man was being kicked off the ship and was stalling his departure. Police gave him a courtesy ride to a motel room with instructions to be good for the night.

09/22/09: Police investigated a call from a woman who thought her neighbors were having a domestic dispute. An officer investigating the noise was told by the couple that they were only role playing, and were "very much in love."

09/25/09: An officer responded to the downtown area and removed a table and chairs from the middle of Broadway Street.

09/26/09: An officer and public works personnel responded to the downtown area to remove a pile of stuff from the middle of Broadway Street again. The pile included bicycles, benches, a hand truck, and other things.

09/26/09: Cash in the amount of $2,700 was reported stolen from the Harbormaster's office during an overnight break-in.

09/29/09: An officer responded to a report of a man piling chairs up in the middle of Broadway. The officer spoke to the only man in the area, and he stated that he did not know anything about the pile, nor the two previous incidents. The officer cleared the mess, as the man was too intoxicated to be of any assistance.

2016

10/03/09: A black bear was reported up a tree in a residential area. Officers managed to scare the bear out of the tree.

10/05/09: A man called and reported the theft of approximately $10,000 from his home. Several days later the man called back to say he had packed his money away and had just remembered where.

10/11/09: A man called and reported that he had driven his vehicle off the Dyea Road when he lost his brakes. He was not injured. An officer responded and gave the man a ride to his home.

10/21/09: A 911 call reporting a possible 5 a.m. traffic accident was received. Responding officers found a 32-year-old Skagway woman had driven her vehicle into a parked sand truck at the city shops, deploying both air bags in the woman's vehicle. She was subsequently arrested for DUI, and transported to the department where she volunteered a breath sample indicating a .18 BAC. She was cited and released on her promise to appear in court.

10/25/09: Shrimp were reported stolen from shrimp pots tied to the Railroad Dock.

11/21/09: A call was received reporting a broken window at a seasonal restaurant. An officer responded and found that the window had been broken with two large rocks and the building had been entered. It was determined that 2.5 cases of beer, a case of wine and four pony kegs of beer were stolen. Investigating officer followed tracks in the snow but eventually lost them.

11/29/09: A 30-year-old Skagway man reported he had struck a residence on State Street with his pickup truck the night before.

12/08/09: Police were dispatched to a described intoxicated male stumbling down the road walking a dog. Turned out the man was sober, was being towed by a large dog, and was trying to get used to a new leash.

12/12/09: Police were asked to watch for a fight brewing between two high school boys at the Yuletide Ball.

12/24/09: Police took an intoxicated man found sitting on the sidewalk outside the Eagles to his home. They returned to warn the bartender about overserving.

BODY IN TOW –The National Park Service's annual Junior Ranger Day is a fun summer event for the kids. This game involves putting on fire bunker gear and dragging a body dummy across the grass at the Moore Homestead, simulating a real rescue. They also get to put out fake fires.

2010

Dog sleepovers, stolen ivory capers, date nights gone wrong, and fireworks flingers foiled by Facebook.

01/10/10: An officer responded to a man's report that his front door had been kicked open. The door was damaged but nothing was missing from inside the home.

02/14/10: A woman came in and reported that an unknown dog had spent the night at her home. The owner was located through the dog's license and he claimed the pet.

02/22/10: A woman called and reported hearing gunshots. Upon investigation it was discovered that DOT personnel were being trained to haze birds and wildlife off the airport runway.

03/27/10: A man came in and reported that his yearly tab sticker was removed from his license plate, his keys taken, and his vehicle had been moved from its original position. His vehicle had been parked while he was out of town for the last 18 months.

04/02/10: A man reported that his vehicle had been vandalized. The words "you are dumb" were scratched into the passenger side window. Two young suspects were identified and their parents contacted.

04/06/10: A woman called and reported that she hit and killed a coyote with her car. The coyote was picked up and disposed of.

Best of the Skagway Police Blotter

04/12/10: A man came in and reported that some time over the winter his unregistered bike was stolen from company housing. He saw the bike and contacted the person riding it. He was told that the bike was found and now registered in the rider's name.

04/18/10: Police made a late night stop on a 24-year-old Skagway man for driving without taillights. Both the driver and his 20-year-old passenger were intoxicated. The driver agreed to provide a breath sample to police, which indicated a .14 BAC. The driver was cited for DUI and furnishing alcohol to a minor, the passenger, who blew a .07 BAC and was cited for minor in possession of alcohol.

04/21/10: An officer responded to a report of damage done to a hotel room. Apparently the hotel guest had come in quite intoxicated and trashed the room. He agreed to pay for all damage done to the room.

04/22 to 4/23/10: An officer assisted a man who had locked his keys in his vehicle. The next day, an officer assisted the man for same issue at a different location.

04/26/10: A subject was observed urinating on a vehicle and then assaulted the resident who reported him. Charging documents were forwarded on the 55-year-old Skagway man, the victim's father-in-law.

04/30/10: Police were called to administer a breathalyzer to a commercial pilot who just landed in Skagway and was suspected of being under the influence. The breath sample indicated a .017 BAC.

05/03/10: Police were unable to locate suspicious persons reported climbing down ladders on the Railroad Dock.

05/16/10: While patrolling Dyea Road, an officer observed a set of vehicle tracks that led toward a steep sloping drop-off. At the end of said tracks was a small unoccupied pickup resting where it collided dead center against a large tree. The officer located the injured driver at a neighboring residence. An ambulance was dispatched to check on her.

05/23/10: Police received a call that someone may be at the liquor store buying alcohol for minors. Later officers cited four underage Canadian youths for minor in possession of alcohol, and a 21-year-old Whitehorse man for furnishing alcohol to minors.

05/28/10: A man reported there was a cat in his yard that looked like it was in bad shape. An officer responded and picked up the cat. Upon research of reports of missing cats, the owner was located in Whitehorse. She had lost her cat in Skagway on April 10. She drove to Skagway and claimed her lost pet.

06/07/10: A woman reported that her car had been vandalized. Someone had written on a bumper sticker on her vehicle with a permanent marker, ruining it.

06/08/10: EMS personnel and police officers responded to a report of a single vehicle accident on the Dyea Road. There were two occupants in the vehicle at the time of the accident, and they both left the vehicle and went to a nearby home for help. Both the driver and passenger were taken by ambulance to the clinic.

06/08/10: An officer responded to a complaint of a person mowing a lawn after 10 p.m. The man was asked to not mow this late in the evening.

06/10/10: An officer responded to assist NPS Rangers with three intoxicated campers at the campground creating a disturbance.

06/10/10: A woman called and reported that someone had shoplifted an ivory statue from the shop where she worked. She believed that the theft took place two days prior. Value of the sculpture is $5,280.

SPIRIT BEAR – This white-phased black bear was the darling of Skagway during the 2007 and 2008 summer seasons, until he was shot by a property owner during an unfortunate incident. Protection for these type bears was sought by local residents, but the Alaska Board of Game had trouble coming up with an enforceable definition. A white cub from this bear's line was relocated to a glacier west of Skagway the following summer to protect the bear. – *Andrew Cremata*

Best of the Skagway Police Blotter

06/10/10: A 28-year-old Skagway man was stopped for failing to stay in his lane of travel. Appearing intoxicated, the man was transported to the department, where he supplied a breath sample indicating a BAC of .19. He was cited for DUI and released on his promise to appear for court.

06/11/10: A man called from Juneau reporting that he had just spoken to his girlfriend via her cell phone. She told him that she was lost here in Skagway and then her phone died. The woman was located and given a ride home.

06/11/10: A woman called and reported that unknown persons had entered her home overnight. She heard footsteps coming upstairs when she called out. The people immediately left the home. She was advised to call 911 immediately if this happened again and not to wait until morning.

KLONDIKE HO! – After enduring more than a month of hardships on the Chilkoot Trail, including having four of their crew flown out for medical attention after eating poisonous plants, the stampeder reenactors for the French Canadian program "La Ruee Vers L'Or" ("The Gold Rush") hit stormy Lake Bennett with two rafts and finally passed through Carcross above on July 14. They reached Whitehorse a few days later and made it to Dawson a month later for Discovery Days. – *Kathleen O'Daniel*

06/12/10: Fire personnel were dispatched for an EWS (early warning system) fire alarm at a local hotel. The alarm had been activated due to water getting into the system caused by a bathtub overflowing.

06/15/10: A woman reported that yesterday before going to dinner she put her $425 camera on the charger in her hotel room. When she came back from dinner her camera was missing.

06/15/10: A carved mammoth tusk was shoplifted from a gallery downtown. The owner suspected the sculpture, which was about a foot wide and 16 inches tall, disappeared in one of three blue shopping bags carried by three female shoppers. A check of the cruise ships revealed all three ships had blue shopping bags today. Ship security was asked to watch for the tusk, valued at $2,900.

06/16/10: A woman reported losing a ring downtown. It was found the next morning and mailed to her.

06/20/10: Officers, Search and Rescue, and EMS personnel were dispatched to a report of a person screaming for help near the Dewey Lakes Trail. Police located a 23-year-old seasonal worker who said she had been attacked by her boyfriend, and that he had a gun. She later admitted to police she had lied about the incident.

06/23/10: EMS personnel were dispatched to the Chilkoot Trail via helicopter for four people on a film shoot who had eaten some poisonous plants. They were brought to the clinic and later transported to Whitehorse by ambulance.

06/24/10: A set of redwood stairs for a hot tub was reported stolen.

06/27/10: Police observed a 26-year-old seasonal worker from Florida walking (poorly) around downtown late at night and gave her a courtesy ride home. Moments later they watched a vehicle leave the area, and stopped the woman from driving. She was transported to the department where she consented to providing a breath sample, which indicated a .15 BAC. She was cited for DUI and driving on a suspended license for unpaid tickets in Florida and Alabama.

06/28/10: A 12-pound walrus ivory sculpture was reported stolen from a gallery. Retail value is $2,975.

06/28/10: An officer was dispatched for a report of two people sleeping on the sidewalk in a residential area. The individuals were awakened and given a ride to their campsite.

06/29/10: Two reports of theft were reported in the downtown area: 1) an ivory bead necklace with an Eskimo artifact pendant valued at $360; 2) an uncarved ivory tusk valued at $2,000.

07/01/10: A woman called and reported that another woman stole her purse while she was using a public restroom. The suspect had blond hair and a pink coat.

07/03/10: A man called and reported that there was a dog in his apartment and he does not have a dog. The dog was picked up and released to its owner.

Best of the Skagway Police Blotter

07/04/10: A 16-year-old male was issued a citation for underage drinking.

07/04/10: A woman called and reported that she had left her purse in a restaurant which was now closed but she could see her purse inside. The owner was contacted and he let the woman in to retrieve her purse.

07/06/10: An officer was dispatched for the report of a shoplifter downtown. After a review of surveillance tapes the shoplifter was located. He was told to return and pay for the $50 gloves.

07/07/10: Officers responded to a report of an unruly passenger on a tour bus. Officer removed them from the bus.

07/09/10: An intoxicated man called and reported that his wife had stolen his children and was headed for the border. This report was unfounded, the woman and children returned while he was still on the phone with the dispatcher.

07/10/10: An officer responded to several reports of a vehicle that had driven off the Klondike Highway. The driver had left the vehicle and was being treated for his injuries at the clinic prior to the reports being called in.

07/11/10: An officer responded to another accident that had happened overnight. The driver reportedly fell asleep and rolled his vehicle.

07/12/10: A woman called and reported her vehicle stolen. It was determined that a co-worker had used the car instead of a company vehicle.

07/14/10: An officer responded to a downtown bar to a report of an unruly customer who had thrown a ketchup bottle at the bartender.

07/17/10: A woman reported dropping her cell phone on the boardwalk and the battery fell between the boards. Public Works was contacted and was able to retrieve the battery.

07/22/10: A report of a possible plane crash on Mt. Harding turned out to be an illusion of rocks and fog.

07/26/10: An officer responded to a reported theft at Liarsville. Two female performers had been skimming gold from the pans. Approximately $6,000 in gold dust was recovered.

08/06/10: Officers were dispatched to the Ferry Terminal in reference to a stolen vehicle. Passengers who just arrived on the ferry climbed into the wrong vehicle, mistaking it for their rental. Taken car was located at the lodge in Dyea, and the cars were switched back around.

08/07/10: A shop owner reported she had followed two shoplifters out of her store and recovered her merchandise. She wanted police to be on the lookout for more incidents.

08/09/10: Officers were dispatched to a disorderly conduct complaint of an intoxicated man refusing to leave a bar. Police took his keys from him and allowed him to sleep it off in his car. Police were called on another man loitering in the Westmark lobby. He too was allowed to sleep it off in his car after police took his keys.

08/13/10: A theft of three planters from the train depot was reported by a woman who saw two people carrying the planters toward a cruise ship. The officer was unable to locate the suspects but was able to retrieve the planters.

08/14/10: Several calls were received regarding an injured animal near Pullen Pond. The reports varied: otter, mink, weasel, or bear. The injured animal was actually a marten, and he managed to take care of himself and went back into his hole.

08/16/10: Officers responded to a report of a window being broken at a bar. A 29-year-old Skagway man had been asked to leave the bar and was being escorted out by employ-

GREEN GIANTS – Jack Inhofe, top, dropped by the editor's house with a huge King Boletus mushroom that he found under a rock by Seven Pastures. He said he will use it to make two pizzas and have enough left over for a half gallon of dried delicacies. Bottom, Evan Sterling was crowned Skagway's first Rhubarb King at a 2009 event at Jewell Gardens.

Best of the Skagway Police Blotter

ees when he struck the door window with his fist as he went.

08/18/10: A man called and reported that he ran over a bike in front of the post office. The owner of the bike was located and information was exchanged with the man who ran over the bike.

08/29/10: A man called and reported that there was a man trying to enter his home. When an officer responded, he found that the man trying to enter the home had a date earlier in the evening with one of the caller's roommates and he showed up late. His date had gotten tired of waiting and she went to bed. He thought the date should still happen. It did not.

09/04/10: Police responded to a reported early morning domestic dispute at the ferry terminal. A 44-year-old Haines woman was arrested for two counts of violation of conditions of release. She was awaiting trial for DUI, 4th degree assault, interfering with a report of domestic violence, and refusal to submit to a chemical test, all stemming from an incident in Haines on July 2.

09/06/10: An officer responded to a downtown business after the manager complained of some customers bad-mouthing the business in front of the building. The customers had a complaint about their purchase and did not feel as if the manager was taking care of it properly.

09/08/10: An officer responded to a cruise ship to investigate a death on board. The 61-year-old Idaho man apparently died of natural causes.

09/15/10: An officer responded to assist a woman near the boat harbor who seemed to be lost. She was trying to get to Haines. An agent from Cruise Line Agencies was contacted and helped her get back to her ship in Haines. She was reported missing by her husband later, and he was told that she was on-board the ship in Haines.

09/17/10: A burglary was reported at the Recreation Center. According to the surveillance video, an unknown male entered the building just after midnight and took cash from the register, a personal iPod, and smashed the glass on the vending machine, taking jerky and gummy snacks.

09/21/10: An officer responded to a report of fireworks being set off. The persons setting off the fireworks were issued a warning and told to stop.

09/21/10: Police were called on a 31-year-old Skagway woman who refused to leave a bar. When

"BOX OF ROCKS" SHOW – Each September, a bunch of Skagwegians head up to Upper Dewey Lake and time themselves in the annual "Box of Rocks" race. The name comes from the simple fact that you have be dumber than a ... to do this. But at least you get a helicopter ride down. During this 2010 event, those who made it to the top were entertained by local musicians who were staying at the cabin for the weekend.

asked, she told police she wouldn't leave, and tried to fight with the officer when he attempted to escort her out. She was arrested for trespass, and continued to fight with the officer while he tried to lodge her for the night in a holding cell.

09/23/10: A man reported that he loaned some camping gear to a man to use for a few weeks, and the man left town with the gear.

09/23/10: A suspicious person was reported being seen going into the dugout at the school ball field. When contacted by the officer, he was found to be drinking and was told that he could not have alcohol in that area. He went home.

Best of the Skagway Police Blotter

10/08/10: A Colt .45 handgun was found by maintenance workers alongside the Klondike Highway and brought to the police department.

10/09/10: A woman reported there was a cat trapped in the walls at her house. It had wandered in and her cat roughed it up. The cat was hiding and would not come out. After a while she managed to get the cat out and returned home.

10/13/10: Officers responded to a report of a black bear by the Westmark. The bear was climbing up the outside wall and had damaged a window in the process. The bear was hazed with a rubber bullet.

10/17/10: A 400-pound brown bear was killed by hunters near City Hall. Police had received many calls of the bear roaming town the past couple of weeks.

10/30/10: Police received many noise complaints about late night fireworks, but were unable to catch anybody firing them off. The next day a local 16-year-old female bragged on her Facebook account how she was responsible for waking the entire town. Police conducted a traffic stop on the student and located a truck full of fireworks, for which she was cited for.

10/30/10: A woman called and reported that when she came to work in the morning she found a man sleeping in the company vehicle. She told him to move on.

10/31/10: A man reported that his business was vandalized. Someone had poured cooking oil at the front and back entrances of his business. Police questioned a neighbor who has had a running feud with the business over late night noise, who admitted to the damage and advised he would clean it up.

11/01/10: An officer assisted a woman whose dog had locked her out of her vehicle.

11/04/10: An officer assisted a man whose dog had locked him out of his vehicle.

11/14/10: Seven shrimp pots were removed from the water near the RR dock. They were all unmarked, but four of them were later claimed. Residents were reminded to properly mark their pots.

11/5 to 12/4/10: Several more reports of bears getting into garbage and police chasing them away until the snow flew and the bears went to sleep.

Heard on the Wind

The wind doth blow and it will bring...

Standing across from Eagles, a tourist watched the girls in windows prior to Days of '98 show for a bit, then turned to a shopkeeper and asked shyly, "they're not really...you know?"

It was explained to him the women were actors, not...anything else. – 05/26/06

A dishwasher at a restaurant was asked by a patron which was the men's and which was the women's rest room.

"They're unisex," the worker replied.

"Is that an Indian word? – 05/26/06

A train crew member overheard this at the back end of the train: "Sit in the last car. You get a longer ride." And then at the other end, behind the engines: "Ride in the front car because the engines are heavier and they won't fall off the track like the back cars." – 05/26/06

Two middle-aged women were studying the program schedule at the National Park Visitor Center. One said, "Look, they have a free movie, and ranger-guided historical walking tours."

"Forget it," replied the second woman. "I don't need that much knowledge." – 06/09/06

Overheard in the Stowaway garden:

Man: "All the light up here makes everything grow really big."

Woman: "Well, I'm buying my husband a one-way ticket and he can't come back until it's huge!"

– 06/09/06

A local guy walking into the Alaska Shirt Co. behind a group of tourists overheard this from a woman: "I sure hope I can find a shirt in here with Alaska printed on it." – 06/23/06

HEARD ON THE WIND

A man asked a tour agent where he could get an Alaska license plate, but after he was told he could buy a sample one downtown, the man asked, "Can't I just take one off a car?"

"That would be stealing," the agent replied.

"No it wouldn't," the man insisted.

"Just don't take it off my car." – 06/23/06

EGGCELLENT – Tanner Hanson and Mike Healy, champs of the 2008 Fourth of July Egg Toss, show off their winning egg, which survived a final toss of 300 feet. Skagway set the Guinness World Record for the number of people in an egg toss that July 4th with an official total of 1,162.

On a tour up to Carcross to see the wildlife museum, a tour guide mentioned the woolly mammoth found in the area.

One genius sitting in the front inquired, "Did they shoot it locally?" – 07/14/06

At the Fourth of July Egg Toss contest, a woman standing behind a man getting ready to catch, asked "Can you catch?"

"Yeah" he said.

Seconds later they were both drenched in egg.

"I thought you said you could catch!" she said.

"I did. My friend can't throw." – 07/14/06

"There's too many jewelry stores and not enough bars." – 07/14/06

A husband and wife were walking and talking.

"Why are there SO MANY Canadian flags here?"

"I think because we are at White Pass, Yukon." – 07/28/06

Overheard from visitors who were walking back to the ship: "Next week we're going on the helicopter and whale ride." – 07/28/06

Four "well fed" people were fast-walking in the direction of the cruise ships about 5:30 p.m., obviously in a hurry for something. The woman in front said, over her shoulder, "Well, you don't want to waste your money by not eating." – 07/28/06

HEARD ON THE WIND

As the narrator on the train was pointing out the Carmack Glacier, sitting some 5,000 feet up the mountain, one older woman turned to her friend and said: "Look, that's what the Titanic hit." – 08/11/06

"Are those the bones of all the dead horses on the front of the building?" asked a person looking up at AB Hall. – 08/11/06

"We're taking the Skagway train today. Does it go to Denali?" – 8/25/06

As a Skaguay Alaskan newsie tried to give a paper to a gentlemen on the Broadway Dock, the man responded, "I think you gave one to my wife. Do you know where she went?" – 08/25/06

"This place ain't much of a frontier. It's got a Starbucks." – 08/25/06

An exchange between two Skagway women canoeing on Nares Lake last weekend near Carcross:
"Do you see the salt lick way up there on the mountain? The goats love it."
"Did they fly it in there?" – 09/08/06

"The reason that the railroad doesn't go to Whitehorse anymore is because they had so much trouble with the bears constantly digging up the tracks." – 09/08/06

A woman on a tour said she went whale watching in Juneau yesterday and the weather was "just as nice on the lake" as it was in Skagway yesterday.
"We saw some hunchback whales," she said. – 09/22/06

Overheard from a tourist asking the proprietor of the Back Alley Rock Shop, "Is it too far to walk to the Tanzanite mine?" – 09/22/06

"How far is it to Fairbanks?" a visitor asked
"I'm not sure but you can ask across the street at the visitor center," replied the clerk.
"You don't know the distance to the next town?" – 09/22/06

"How long have you been here?"
"Fifteen years."
"And you look so normal." – 09/22/06

HEARD ON THE WIND

A woman called the visitor center wanting to know "What is the temperature of the ground in July?" so she can decide how thick the soles of her shoes should be when she comes to visit. –05/11/07

"Look honey, stamps are the same price here as they are back home." –05/11/07

A dog without a leash and its owner walked right past a police officer, in uniform.
"Excuse me," the officer said. "We have a leash law in this town."
The owner showed the officer a rope in her hand.
"Why aren't you using it?" the officer asked.
"My dog's a free spirit."
She was told how much a ticket cost and put the rope on her dog. –05/11/07

"Do you have snakes in the water up here? There's all these little things sticking up out of the water with little heads on them," said a visitor, who still did not believe he was seeing otters from the deck of his stateroom, several stories above the water. – 06/08/07

A guy walks into the Back Alley Rock Shop and says "Oh dude, this is a real rock shop, man. I was looking for a poster of Lynyrd Skynyrd, man." – 06/08/07

People are really worried about how they look these days....
"So why do you think they built the railroad as a narrow gauge?"
"People were slimmer back in 1898." – 06/22/07

Woman posing for picture between the totems on 5th Ave: "If I stand next to this totem does it make me look fat?" – 06/22/07

While walking home, a couple heard this exchange:
Husband: "I still just don't see how people actually live here."
Wife: "Well, I don't think they do." – 06/22/07

After one head-on encounter with a grizzly walking straight down the middle of the trail, and stepping by four piles of bear droppings on the trail, one lady asked her guide, "Do the bears use the trail?"
– 06/22/07

80

HEARD ON THE WIND

On a tour to and from the lookout, a visitor noticed that a police car with a radar gun had not moved. "What's up with that?" he said. "You don't have any donut shops in town?" – 06/22/07

"How long can a salmon hold its breath?"
"These mosquitoes sure are friendly, aren't they?" – 07/06/07

A woman in the visitor center was disappointed that the ship was unable to get into Tracy Arm to see the glaciers calving, and was told that the glaciers are melting more quickly now and in some cases disappearing from view.
She opined, "Oh well, maybe there will be some new ones soon." – 07/06/07

"Will we be back in time for our ship's aurora borealis show?"
"Where can I find one of those aurora borealis stones?" – 07/20/07

From the political division: Senator Lisa Murkowski recently hiked the Chilkoot Trail with a group of friends and family. On her train ride from Lake Bennett, she remarked about the contrast of her trail experience compared with what she had to do the next day in D.C., which was a meeting with Hillary Clinton. A WP&YR crew member summed it up for her this way, "So, you're going from bear bait to de-bate." – 07/20/07

A people mover driver on the dock was asked by a passenger. "So how much farther does Puget Sound go?"
"Ma'am," he replied. "Puget Sound is in Washington state."
"We're not in Washington anymore?!" – 08/10/07

A teenage boy and girl were trying to grab salmon out of Pullen Creek. The boy was finally successful, only for a few seconds, holding up a 5-pounder by the tail.
His sister, in an authentic Alaska raccoon skin cap, exclaimed, " Let it go, you're choking it to death!" – 08/24/07

A hotel guest asked if the water temperature on the clothes washing machine was marked in Celsius or Fahrenheit. She was told it was marked "Hot" and "Cold." – 08/24/07

A woman walked into a store to purchase some warmer clothing, complaining that she didn't realize it was going to be so cold here.

HEARD ON THE WIND

The clerk explained to her that she was quite far north, and asked why she thought it would be warm here.

The visitor replied, "Well, it's right next to Hawaii on the map." – 08/24/07

A boy of about 4 asked the adult he was walking with: "Is it okay to step on the cracks in a boardwalk?" 09/07/07

A couple asked, "When is high tide? We've been in every port in Alaska and we've never seen it." They were advised it changed every day, and they conceded that must be why they missed it. –09/07/07

Heard at the '98 Show: "What time is the 10:30 show?" – 09/07/07

From the street: "I understand the Gold Rush, but when did the Diamond Rush begin?"
Another commented: "Skagway should build a mall for all their shops. That would keep all the people off the boardwalk and more room to walk." – 05/30/08

From the gallery: A clerk explained to a customer, "This is all mammoth ivory here."
"Mammoths aren't endangered, are they?" the customer asked.
"Worse, they're extinct." – 05/30/08

From the read into this what you will department: A local man walked into a store and observed an oosik and remarked, "How did it get so shiny? I rub and polish mine at home and it never gets that shiny." ¬– 06/13/08

From the power dudes at AP&T: A woman walked into the police department and had a formal complaint about a man, in a chair, covered in a sheet up in the power lines. The woman was told that the local telephone company was doing work on the lines and everything is OK. The lady complained that it just wasn't right. Apparently, the workers with hard hats on, and the road blocked off by an AP&T boom truck was not enough to convince this woman that we know what we are doing. –06/13/08

A visitor was inquiring about "Carrot Cross." When told it is actually Carcross and short for Caribou Crossing, he asked if caribou eat carrots. "Well, no, they actually eat grass."
"Well, then why is it called Carrot Cross?" – 06/30/08

HEARD ON THE WIND

From Mendenhall Glacier in Juneau:
"What happens to the white color when the snow melts?"
"How do you tell the difference between a fresh salmon and a smoked salmon?"
"Can you fish through the glacier?" – 07/11/08

A gentleman walked into Jewell Gardens housing break room and asked the location of the "seal show."

He explained that he had been told to walk across the bridge and there would be a seal show. "Where is it?"

He was directed to the footbridge a mile to the south and told to look out for them at Yakutatnia Point.

From the deep, dark waters: A tourist asked a bartender at the Elks, what kind of "spider" was hanging on the wall.

The bartender looked up at the handsome wall mount of a creature from the depths of Taiya Inlet, and said, "That's an Alaskan King Crab spider." – 07/11/08

COMMUNITY ROCK GARDEN? – Several residents on June 18, 2006 began work on the new community garden north of the school ballfield. City crews removed cottonwoods from the property to make room for garden beds. Most of the first day's work was spent digging up rocks, but they said the soil looked good. Bob Fink, above, boasted the biggest rock pile.

Profiling locals: A visitor asked a clerk, "Are you from here?
She replied, "Yes."
"Well, you don't look like you're from here." – 07/25/08

HEARD ON THE WIND

A lady was looking at salt and pepper shakers in a shop. When told they were made of caribou antler, she exclaimed, "You have caribou in Alaska?!" – 07/25/08

After looking at "Mickey Moose" shirts, a visitor seemed confused.
"So what is a moose like, kind of like a mouse?"
"No, more like a horse."
"Oh," the visitor replied. "Can you pet one?" – 07/25/08

Customer: "Where can I find wolves?"
Clerk: "Excuse me?"
Customer: "You know, WOLVES. Could I find one in town? At a reservation or something?"
Clerk: "No."
Customer: "Oh. They like to hide. What about moose? Do they like to hide too?" – 08/15/08

A bear was spotted peeking through the bushes while guests were eating at Liarsville Salmon Bake. A woman asked, "Is it real?" – 08/15/08

Heard on a D.A.T. bus: "At what elevation does a caribou become a moose?"
Heard on the Ore Dock: A very confused lady said, "All of the signs around here say 'White Pass' but my ticket is yellow –Where do I go?" – 08/29/08

We speak English, eh… Visitor from Texas: "Along the panhandle where Alaska meets Canada, do people speak both English and Canadian?" – 09/12/08

A couple was looking at the outgoing mail slots at the post office and seemed confused.
One stopped in front of the "Out of Town" slot and said to the other: "I don't know. We've been here all summer."
Her partner replied: "Maybe we should put it in 'Local?'" – 09/12/08

A group of visitors coming off the Broadway Dock pulled out their cameras to catch a rainbow rising over near Dyea. One of them exclaimed, "I better get back to the casino!" – 09/26/08

Oh, Governor: A visitor was overheard asking a local where one might find pictures of Sarah Palin in a bathing suit. – 09/26/08

2011

A daring mountain rescue, snow drifters, phone booth thievery, crazed crows on the attack, unauthorized sleepovers, rogue wolf destroyed, alleged affair and extraction from ship, and many intoxicated wanderers.

01/04/11: Police found a car stuck in a Dyea Road ditch. The driver was unharmed, the car was freed with the help of a heavy equipment operator, and police escorted the driver home.

01/05/11: Eight members of Skagway's SAR (Search and Rescue) team responded to Haines to help rescue a man who had fallen in a ravine on Mt. Rapinsky and couldn't get out.

01/20/11: An early morning momentary power outage set off Christmas music blaring inside the White Pass Depot, requiring management to respond and silence it.

01/28/11: Police received a report of timber theft on Dyea Road. The thief left behind a red bow saw, small red gas can, bar oil, and a hand truck.

01/28/11: The male half of a Spring Street household called dispatch and asked if police could escort his intoxicated female half off the property. Caller, who was hiding in the garage with the lights off, told police to be on guard as she was in a bad mood.

02/07/11: After the owner accidently ran over his dog, police helped the man get the injured dog from the Gold Rush Cemetery road to the animal impound, where responders from Paws and Claws tried to help the pet.

Best of the Skagway Police Blotter

02/27/11: An officer needed assistance after he got his patrol car stuck in a snow drift in an alley. A second officer responded and helped dig out the car. A resident also got his vehicle stuck in a snow drift on 16th Avenue and needed an officer to help set him free.

02/28/11: A skylight was found in the middle of Broadway Street. Police determined it blew off of the Shirt Company building, and advised the winter caretaker.

02/28/11: The clinic called dispatch and advised they were treating an apparent stabbing victim. Police responded, and the victim said that the night before he had been stabbed in the back by an unknown woman wearing a full ski mask and pushed to the ground in front of a Broadway Street bar that he had been drinking at. The wound took several stitches. After police investigated the incident further, the man admitted to police that the wound was self-inflicted and that he made the story up.

03/30/11: A returning seasonal businessman reported that sometime over the winter someone stole a red, full-size, antique telephone booth from outside his shop. Police found a witness who said he saw somebody with a fork lift take the phone booth from the property two or three weeks prior, however the current whereabouts of the phone booth were unknown.

04/19/11: A Dyea Road resident called police after she received a call asking her to remove her van from alongside the railroad tracks near the Dewey Lakes trailhead. She told police that last she knew her husband had left the van at the airport. Police found the van unlocked, the keys in the ignition, and the headlight switch on. Inside was a dog collar with a local 2010 dog license. The dog license came back to a local man known to the van owner. She did not wish to press charges, and would take it up with the man why her van had been removed from the airport and abandoned by the railroad tracks.

05/12/11: A vehicle with loose lug nuts lost a wheel in front of the Post Office. Officers responded to provide traffic control and asked that the Fire Department respond with equipment to get the wheel back on the vehicle. Prior to FD arrival, a citizen arrived with a floor jack and the vehicle was repaired.

05/20/11: Dispatch received a call from the Dyea campground where a woman's child was locked in their truck camper. The child was fine – she could see him through the window – and she hoped police could locate her husband. An officer was able to, and sent him back to Dyea with a camper key.

05/22/11: A caller said he heard an automobile crash on the Dyea Flats and when he went to the scene he saw someone run into the woods. The vehicle's front bumper was broken in two and the airbags were deployed. Responding officers made contact with a 21-year-old Palmer man near the Taiya River Bridge and issued citations for reckless driving and leaving scene of accident.

06/01/11: Dispatch received a call of a possible missing person. The hiker is a 62-year-old male who hikes to Lower Lake every day, and was about four hours overdue to return. An officer headed over to the Brew Co. to make sure the hiker had not stopped off on the way home, and in fact found the overdue hiker inside.

06/03/11: Police spoke to rangers regarding the crows nesting in a park service tree and attacking passersby on Broadway Street. NPS will have personnel stationed until 6 p.m. warning people about the birds.

06/07/11: Officers responded to provide traffic control on Congress Way where a train had derailed and all passengers were unloading.

06/09/11: A caller reported a mean three-legged terrier type dog in the area of 20th and State that was loose and growling and charging at people. An officer responded but was unable to locate any mean three-legged dogs in the area.

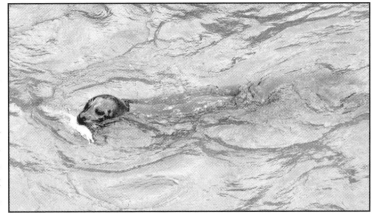

SALMON SNATCHER – A seal parades with his catch near the Pullen Creek outfall by the Broadway Dock. – *Mark Adabi*

06/12/11: Police stopped a 22-year-old Skagway man for erratic driving, and arrested same for driving under the influence. At the station he decided not to provide a sample of his breath. He was cited on both charges and released on his promise to appear for court.

06/18/11: Police received a report of an intoxicated female bicyclist crashing into a parked car. Officers located a foot-long scratch on the car but were unable to locate the bicyclist.

06/19/11: At about 1:40 a.m. police were contacted by a woman who had been involved in an altercation at the Bonanza. She did not want to press charges, but she did ask officers for a ride home. Less than an hour later officers were called to the Bonanza to investigate late night vandalism. Noted in the men's bathroom was a dented waste bin and paper towel holder, holes in walls, broken stall doors, and drains kicked off the bottom of all three sinks. Outside the bar several bicycles had also been damaged, suffering from broken spokes and bent rims. Shortly thereafter someone pulled a fire alarm on an outside wing of the Westmark. Witnesses reported seeing suspects run down Congress Way toward the Railroad Dock. An officer on 3 a.m. patrol noticed two men inside the Fish Co and wondered if they were supposed to be in there at that hour. The men refused to open the door for the officer, and when dispatch contacted the owner he said nobody should be inside. Other officers responded, and the owner showed up with a key. Officers noticed a crawl space door over the kitchen was ajar, and three men were removed from the ceiling crawl space. All were employees and the owner did not want to press charges. Reasons for refusing to come to door and hiding are unknown, although one man did admit to pulling the fire alarm outside the hotel.

06/19/11: A 31-year-old Louisiana man told police that he needed to get out of Skagway because people were after him. He was furnished with a ferry ticket to Juneau.

06/21/11: The Bonanza called after a women threw drug paraphernalia at the bartender and then went into the ladies room and would not come out. A responding officer found the woman passed out in one of the stalls. The officer woke the woman and gave her a courtesy ride home

06/21/11: A woman called 911 and said she had walked through the back door of a restaurant at Seventh and Broadway Street and was stuck in a little yard out back. All the doors leading back inside the restaurant were locked and she is trapped. She said no one is responding to her knocking on the doors. A responding officer found the woman and reunited her with her husband.

06/23/11: Dispatch received a report of someone yelling for help at the end of the Railroad Dock. The caller said it sounds like it is coming from the very end of it, like the individual was stuck on the rocks. A responding officer failed to hear the cries, however state ferry personnel just leaving the area put out a rescue boat and picked up a 30-year-old male with a head contusion. Rescuers described the man as bleeding but conscious, and brought him into the small boat harbor where he was transferred to the clinic.

06/24/11: A resident on 11th Avenue called and asked for an officer to respond to his house. He had just woken up to find a stranger sleeping on his couch. A responding officer found a 21st Avenue resident on the couch. The two men did not know each other, and the stranger said he did not know where he was. The officer pointed the couch surfer in the right direction.

2011

06/24/11: Dispatch received a call from a gentleman at an RV park reporting an assault. The caller said a large man is beating up on a girl inside a trailer, and that the man is bigger than the caller so he can't do anything. Responding officers ordered the man out of the trailer, and when the man refused he had to be forcibly evicted and restrained. The 43-year-old seasonal worker was transported to the police station and charged with domestic violence assault.

06/27/11: A caller reported that there has been a wolf in Dyea. She said that it killed a dog yesterday and this morning her neighbors were missing a dog and a cat.

06/27/11: Dispatch received a half dozen complaints of illegal camping in the woods between Smuggler's Cove and Yakutania Point. Responding officers located the camps – all unoccupied – and left notes that the campsites would have to be moved to legal RV park sites.

06/30/11: Dispatch received a 911 call that a dog had just been taken by a wolf in Liarsville. The caller told dispatch that the dog owner was on his way to Liarsville with a gun. An officer responded with state biologists who were also in town, however all were unable to locate the wolf.

07/01/11: The owner of the popcorn emporium reported the business had been broken into overnight. An officer responded to investigate, finding that while the small amount of money in the cash drawer had not been taken, the only thing apparently missing were several bags of chocolate-drizzled popcorn.

07/01/11: A patrolling officer reported that he has sighted a wolf on the Klondike Highway near the Dyea Road cut off. A NPS ranger and a state biologist responded to the area, where the wolf was shot and killed.

07/03/11: Personnel at the ferry terminal requested additional security for the ferry tonight, especially around fireworks time. Apparently last year the ship had been struck by flung bottles.

07/03/11: A visitor reported the bank ATM dispensed $300 and a check card that did not belong to him. Dispatch tracked the owner of the card and cash back to a cruise ship.

07/04/11: A visitor reported that while she was attending the parade this morning, she discovered someone in the parade threw candy and apparently her ring came off while the candy was being thrown. The visitor turned over a gold band with gold nuggets surrounding a purple gemstone. The dispatcher recognized the ring, and called the local owner who was very thankful it had been recovered.

Best of the Skagway Police Blotter

07/04/11: An officer with Carcross RCMP called SPD and requested an officer's assistance in picking up a cruise ship passenger who had crashed a rental Jeep near the Fraser, BC border station in Canada. They were processing the driver for DUI, and he would need to be retrieved and taken back to the States. Dispatch located the owner of the Jeep Tours and told them their wrecked Jeep would need to be retrieved, and an officer responded to Fraser and delivered the Pennsylvania man back to his ship.

07/13/11: A local woman called from Anchorage and reported that her vehicle had been stolen from her residence on Alaska Street. A neighbor noticed yesterday that her car was not in its usual parking spot. Police were notified and started to search for the vehicle, when the woman called back and said to never mind, as she had forgot that she parked the vehicle at the airport when she flew out.

07/15/11: Dispatch received a 911 call from an employee who is following two ladies toward town from the Fish Company that left without paying their bill. A responding officer located and escorted all three back to the restaurant where the ladies made good.

07/15/11: A shop owner reported that an employee had resigned but still had two rings valued at approximately $4,000 that don't belong to him that he wore as part of the job. He failed to make it to the exit interview, and as he is scheduled to fly out this evening, she would like an officer at the airport to search his belongings. Instead, an officer located the man and the issue was resolved.

07/21/11: A lady named Maria who said she was from British Columbia reported she was kicked off a cruise ship in Ketchikan last week after being drugged the night before. She said she flew to Skagway and has been staying at a local motel for the past few days. She said she did not contact the police in Ketchikan at the time because she read on the Internet that Alaska will cover for the cruise ships since that is how Alaska makes its money. She said she wanted to get back to Vancouver, and was curious if the fastest way was through Whitehorse via Yakutat. Officers checked around and found that Maria had in fact been removed from a cruise ship in Ketchikan due to her "crazy behavior." From there she flew to Juneau and tried to get back on board the ship and then flew to Skagway with the intent of trying to get back on board. They will not take her back on the ship, and the ship left Skagway yesterday evening.

07/22/11: Dispatch received a phone call from Jim, who is wondering what is going on with his wife, Maria. Dispatch advised him that his wife left on the ferry this morning. Jim mentioned that he has contacted the cruise line to try to figure out why his wife was kicked off the ship. He thinks that his wife is having an affair with the captain and, now that the cat is out of the bag, the captain is afraid he might lose his job.

2011

07/26/11: Police received a complaint about a man hitting golf balls across the river from Yakutania Point. The caller heard a golf ball hit one of Petro Marine's oil tanks. Police responded and told the man to stop.

07/29/11: Police cited two men for having a non-permitted fire at a campsite above the "clock" on the cliffs. Near the fire, a tent completely covered/sheltered with sticks and small logs was discovered. One of the men denied knowing anything about the covert tent even after officers found paperwork with his name on it inside.

07/31/11: Officers responded to the Bonanza where a large group of people were outside arguing. All stated that they were "just trying to protect a girl from a drunk guy." The "drunk guy" left the area before officers arrived, and nobody could describe him.

08/02/11: A caller reported that a person just walked into the culvert under Congress Way. Responding officers were unable to locate anyone in culvert.

08/02/11: White Pass called and requested an officer meet an incoming train. Two people were reportedly involved in an altercation on board. The responding officer discovered that it was two families fighting and that no further action was taken.

08/06/11: Police received a report of a 67-year-old cruise ship passenger who was overdue from a Lower Lake hike. His wife was very concerned since he is never late, and the ship was scheduled to leave port in a couple of hours. Two officers headed up the trailhead while the fire department checked bars and restaurants. After an hour of searching, the ship advised that the man was safely back on the ship and in fact had returned just minutes after the initial report.

08/14/11: Police received a 2 a.m. report of a forklift being driven in circles in the market parking lot. An intoxicated man was discovered walking in the area. He admitted to driving the forklift, and once transported to the station he blew a .130 BAC. Due to a myriad of circumstances, he was released on his promise to be good and leave the country in the morning.

08/14/11: The clandestine long-term campsite of a summer employee was discovered near Yakutania Point. The camping gear was confiscated, and the owner cited when he showed up at the police department to retrieve it.

Best of the Skagway Police Blotter

08/14/11: A shop owner presented police with security video of a cruise ship member stealing an iPhone from his store. Police met with ship security when the ship returned a week later, the thief was identified (and fired by the cruise line), and the iPhone returned.

08/15/11: Police received several calls on an intoxicated woman harassing patrons and refusing to leave when asked by the bartender. Responding officers were unable to find a room at the inn for her, and instead had dispatch notify RCMP that they would be escorting her to Canadian Customs for release.

08/18/11: A shop owner reported they had a thief in custody. She observed the male suspect go into the dressing room with two shirts and come out empty handed. He was stopped in front of the store and confronted and confessed to stealing two shirts that were found in his backpack. The officer took custody of the foreign summer resident and transferred him to U.S. Customs for processing. Customs will revoke the man's immigration status and order him out of country.

SANTA TRAIN – The annual Santa Train is a big event during Skagway's month-long Yuletide celebration.

– Katie Emmets

08/20/11: A resident from Seventh and Main reported that she just had a highly intoxicated lady on her deck. She attempted to enter through the door – which was locked – at which point the caller told her that she was about to get shot. The lady was last seen wandering off toward Main Street. Police were unable to locate her. Twenty minutes later a resident from 10th and Main called and reported an intoxicated girl had entered his house. A responding officer was able to give her a courtesy ride home and find a roommate to watch her for the night.

08/20/11: Police stopped a 34-year-old Skagway woman for erratic driving. She was transported to the department where a breath sample indicated a .25 BAC. She was cited for DUI and released on her promise to appear for court.

2011

08/23/11: A caller reported that there is a "rather large" intoxicated male staggering toward the Broadway Dock. A responding officer determined that he did not belong near the Broadway Dock at all, and gave the man a ride back to his ship at the Railroad Dock.

08/24/11: Two ladies reported they saw a black wolf while hiking on the Lower Lake Trail.

08/27/11: Police responded to a late night silent alarm at the bank and contacted a man at the ATM whose card had been rejected. When police asked why the silent alarm had been tripped, security said they were not sure, however they noted it may have been tripped by kicking or hitting the machine out of frustration.

08/27/11: A bus driver reported seeing people shooting rifles from the Klondike Highway across the valley at the at the railroad tracks just south of U.S. Customs. A responding officer contacted two locals, who were moved on and agreed not to shoot skeet from the highway.

08/27/11: Two callers complained about smoking inside the Eagles in violation of the recently enacted smoking ban, and demanded that police respond and enforce the law. An officer secured a copy of the new code and delivered it to the bartender and requested she advise her members of the change.

08/28/11: Dispatch received another complaint of people smoking in the Eagles.

08/28/11: Police stopped a vehicle for erratic driving. A combative 39-year-old Skagway woman was transported to the department where she provided a breath sample indicating a .079 BAC. She was cited for driving under the influence of alcohol or drugs and released on her promise to appear for court.

09/01/11: A manager reported that someone had attempted to steal a jewelry case from the Westmark lobby. The electrical cord was cut and everything in the case was askew, however nothing was missing.

09/04/11: A resident from Sixth and Alaska Street called 911 and was twice routed through Hoonah PD dispatch. He had a lady who did not belong in his house sleeping on his couch. An officer responded and moved her along.

09/04/11: The combative 39-year-old Skagway woman arrested earlier for DUI was arrested for felony domestic violence assault after officers responded to a call for help. She had reportedly struck her roommate with a chair, breaking several ribs.

Best of the Skagway Police Blotter

09/05/11: The above Sixth and Alaska resident reported that his bike was stolen from in front of the Red Onion Saloon. He believes the same trespassing lady is the one who took his bike. He also doesn't want to have another episode where he tries calling 911 and gets routed to Hoonah. Dispatch advised the phone company was working on the issue.

09/07/11: A caller reported her vehicle had been vandalized while parked outside her residence near Second and Main Street. She reported the steering wheel was bent and the turn indicator lever was broken off, however small bags of change were untouched.

09/10/11: White Pass reported that a train engine sustained multiple BB hits to a left window. The damage is possibility happening when passing the campground in the morning.

09/11/11: A concerned caller reported that an unidentified male left a neighbor's house this morning smoking a cigarette and leaving the front door open. Dispatch called a family member as the homeowners were out on the road relay. The family member checked and secured the residence.

09/11/11: Caller asked if one of the officers would speak with a neighbor. Reportedly this person continually walks his dog without a leash. Caller has approached him about this and he just ignores her requests to get a leash. Caller's husband spoke with this person and got a tongue-lashing. Caller says that the dog is friendly and has never bothered her, but the owner isn't abiding by the law and continues to walk his dog without a leash.

09/18/11: Police recorded over 100 calls of bears on porches, in yards, in alleys, on streets, in garbage, trying to get in freezers or garages, and generally being a nuisance or concern so far this year. Many of these bears were hazed with cracker or rubber rounds. This week, with the beginning of hunting season, four bears were shot and killed, including one in a yard behind an in-town bed and breakfast after the hunter was called by police.

09/20/11: White Pass called to report that $1,575 had been taken from a tour guide's backpack aboard the Fraser train. At this time they do not have any suspects. The money vanished while the guide was outside the train helping passengers disembark.

09/27/11: Caller asked if an officer would be able to pick up a couple of bags he left on the front porch of his summer residence. An officer retrieved two suitcases and a backpack and delivered them to the airport.

2011

10/01/11: Officers helped a Whitehorse man recover an excavator bucket that had been stolen from Whitehorse and purchased by a local construction company.

10/05/11: Dispatch received a call from a 32-year-old Skagway man who said he was at an Alaska Street residence breaking stuff and he was going to be breaking more stuff. Officers responded, and the man, armed with a knife, challenged the officers to fight. He then spit on an officer twice before he could be restrained, arrested, and charged with harassment and misconduct involving a weapon.

10/15/11: Caller complained about a person walking two dogs without having them on a leash. Caller questioned the person about not having the dogs on a leash and that there is a leash law – and the person just laughed at the caller. A responding officer located and spoke with the violator about keeping her dogs on a leash. Ten minutes later the violator called and complained about a chocolate lab at Pullen Pond that was not on a leash, and a minute later the violator called and complained about a dog sitting in back of a pickup that was not on a leash.

10/15/11: A Main Street resident was contacted and asked to move a piece of heavy equipment that was protruding into street. While at his residence the officer spotted a quarter ounce of marijuana on the kitchen table and the resident agreed to flush it down the toilet.

10/23/11: RCMP called and wanted to know if there were any reports of a missing or stolen red Isuzu Trooper. They had such a vehicle dumped near Jake's Corner, YT with no license plates and the VIN number scratched off. An officer was able to direct them to a hidden VIN that showed the title had been transferred and the vehicle was registered in Skagway two weeks prior. Dispatch advised it appeared the new owner was a summer worker who probably dumped the vehicle on the way out of town.

11/01/11: A patrolling officer observed the side window on a trailer parked in an RV park was pushed open and the inside screen was removed. Inside the trailer nothing appeared to be riffled or taken.

11/24/11: A caller reported he was concerned about what appeared to be a dying orphaned black bear cub on his Dyea property.

11/25/11: An officer responded to a report of possible gunfire near Fifth and Broadway. While patrolling he observed fireworks explode in the area and located two adults drinking beer in an alley. Officer had them pour out the beer (since in the Historic District), and noticed a green fuse protruding from a coat pocket. He confiscated five large fireworks and released the two with a verbal warning.

Best of the Skagway Police Blotter

11/28/11: Dispatch received several calls from Dyea Road residents of big bangs and loud explosions. Officer contacted two men who agreed to stop blowing things up at a tour housing complex.

12/02/11: A resident near 18th and State Street called to file a late afternoon noise complaint. He says blaring music is coming from the open windows of a neighbor's house. The caller thinks his neighbor is on a drinking binge and does not want to talk to him. Dispatch advised that the noise ordinance does not apply until after 10 p.m., however an officer will be advised. A responding officer contacted the neighbor, who agreed to turn the music down.

12/10/11: A caller asked that a dark-clothed man walking up the Klondike Highway in the dark be checked on. A responding officer found the man several miles up the highway, waiving his arms. The officer recognized the highly intoxicated local man, who was belligerent and highly agitated, and told him that drivers would not pick him up. The man insisted that he needed to go north while the officer returned him south to his residence.

12/24/11: A school official reported that he had been called about four high school students who had been drinking at Yakutania Point the night before after purchasing alcohol from a 21-year-old local man. The man was cited for furnishing to minors.

12/31/11: Officers stopped a vehicle for no taillights. Upon contact with the driver, the officer smelled the odor of alcoholic beverage. The driver admitted to consuming several alcoholic beverages, and after a field investigation the 56-year-old Skagway man was arrested for DUI. He was transported to the office where he blew a .10 BAC and was cited and released on his own recognizance. During the arrest the officer reported the man became uncooperative and resistive. His wife, a passenger in the vehicle, loudly challenged the officers and had to be warned repeatedly not to advance or interfere. She reportedly refused to move away as instructed. After her husband was transported to the office, she arrived to wait for him. While one officer carried out the booking procedure, the other officer, who had been challenged on the street, asked her to sign a citation for disorderly conduct. Their 31-year-old daughter was also present in the lobby and reportedly became very loud and aggressive to the point where the dispatcher could not hear radio or phone traffic. After being asked several times to quiet down and to stop interfering with her mother in signing her citation, the daughter was also cited for disorderly conduct. All were eventually released on their signed promises to appear.

2012

Uncooperative tour passengers, garden thieves, very drunk softballers, unruly cruisers, and others caught "goofing off" while police are there to help.

01/16/12: Police investigated a trespass complaint into vacant employee housing on Second Avenue. Apparently somebody had the combination to the lock on the front door, but left through the kitchen window.

01/21/12: Police rescued a driver stranded in the snow up the Klondike Highway and took him to a motel to spend the night.

02/24/12: An injured moose with an apparent broken leg was put down by police near Liarsville on the Klondike Highway.

03/06/12: Police and Fire responded to a structure fire involving a wing of the Westmark Inn. The hotel was currently closed for the season, and the small wing was mainly used for employee housing. Firefighters fought the blaze in high winds and freezing temperatures for almost 12 hours before it was under control. The fire was later determined to be arson, and while police identified and questioned a primary suspect, the man later fled town before an arrest could be made.

03/15/12: Police received several complaints about gunfire emanating from a residence at Fifth and Main Street. Police contacted a very intoxicated man shooting off fireworks. He was told to cease, and was later seen exuberantly dancing in his garage instead.

Best of the Skagway Police Blotter

03/30/12: Dispatch received a report that there was a male lying in the middle of the street at Fourth and State Street. The caller advised the subject was bleeding from his face. Police arrived and the man was transported by EMS to the clinic. After being checked out the man refused further treatment and walked away from the clinic, refusing to cooperate.

05/05/12: A woman reported that she saw two individuals, a male and a female acting suspicious at Mollie Walsh Park. She noticed that they placed something underneath a picnic table, and once they left, she picked up the item – a magnetized box – and brought it down to the PD. A responding officer was able to open the box and found a note inside. The note appeared to be directions to a geo-cache. The woman said she would return the note to the picnic table.

05/07/12: A man reported that a vehicle in his party had broken down near the summit and needed some synthetic oil. Dispatch contacted the hardware store owner who responded and opened after hours to aid the man.

05/10/12: A set of found keys were turned in to the PD. The dispatcher recognized the first name on the key fob, and was able to reunite the keys with their owner.

05/12/12: Officers assisted with a landlord/tenant dispute on Eighth Avenue. The homeowner was unhappy about yard work her tenant had performed and was attempting to evict him over it.

05/13/12: While on patrol an officer noticed a woman walking on the airport tarmac at 1:00 in the morning. Making contact, the officer observed fresh bruises, scratches and cuts on her face, back and arms. Police got her to a safe location, and subsequently arrested a 41-year-old Skagway man for domestic violence.

05/15/12: Police received a report that a key had been left in the door lock at a downtown business. Officers responded and secured the key, which was later retrieved by its owner.

05/20/12: Ambulance and police responded to a person reportedly unresponsive after being fished out of the water at the small boat harbor. The subject had tripped and fell in while trying to maneuver a boat from the dock. He was found to be responsive, and was OK except for being wet and cold.

05/24/12: Police checked and secured five unlocked businesses during after-hours security checks. Three more were checked and secured the next night.

05/26/12: Police contacted six individuals under the Skagway River Bridge with two six packs and a bottle of hard alcohol. Two of the individuals were of drinking age, the others were not. All agreed they would rather pour out the alcohol rather than contend with minor in possession and furnishing to minor charges.

05/28/12: Police searched downtown for a missing lady in a wheel chair. Public Works opened the museum as her husband thought she may have visited there, and passed out inside the restroom. After not finding her, and checking out other restrooms in town, they discovered the woman had made it back to the ship on her own.

05/30/12: Dispatch took two complaints of a raven harassing people near Sixth and Broadway Street. The birds were protecting their nest in a tree, and reportedly scratched one person as he walked by. Dispatch advised this is a problem every year with ravens in that tree, and there's nothing anyone can do except let it run its course.

05/30/12: A bus driver called to complain of a couple of tourists who were causing a disturbance on his bus and refusing to get off. He stated he was trying to transfer them to a different bus so people on the original bus could enjoy their tour. The visitors agreed to change buses before an officer was able to arrive to mediate.

06/02/12: A "pretty steamed" caller reported to police that the Icy Lake Trail had been blocked by 50 or more cut trees. The trail was clear three days ago, but today he took his 4-wheeler up to ride and was treated to the trail being blocked. He moved the trees out of the way so he could continue to ride, and feels that this is the work of "liberal a-holes."

BELLY BOWL I – For a couple of winters, the Skagway Brewing Co. held a belly bumping contest in January before the Super Bowl.

Best of the Skagway Police Blotter

06/03/12: Police contacted a loud intoxicated person near Seventh and Broadway. The gentleman agreed to quiet down, and officers poured out a nearby liquor bottle the man did not wish to claim. Police were later dispatched to the Red Onion where the man was refusing requests to leave. The man left just before police arrival. While searching for the man, police learned that he had also visited the Bonanza, where he had to be removed from the kitchen area and damaged the building before leaving.

06/04/12: Police contacted occupants of a State Street residence after receiving a complaint of people shooting at crows with a BB gun. Shooters were advised to cease and desist.

06/06/12: Three flats of potted petunias (valued at $50 each) were presumably poached overnight from a yard at 15th and State Street.

06/06/12: A jeweler reported that a woman made a $1,100 purchase whilst stealing two diamond bracelets worth $20,000 each. Police reviewed the theft on a store surveillance tape and then went aboard the Norwegian Jewel, where, along with ship's security, they were able to recover the merchandise.

06/08/12: Police responded to a one-car vehicle collision on Dyea Road in which a Ford Ranger pickup was snapped in two after colliding with a boulder on the hillside near Long Bay. A 30-year-old Skagway man was leaning on the rear bumper among many scattered beer cans upon police arrival, suffering from a bump on his forehead corresponding to a dent in the pickup windshield. After failing field sobriety tests, the driver was transported to the police department where he consented to a breath test resulting in a BAC sample of .155. He was cited for DUI and released on his promise to appear.

06/09/12: Broadway Street ravens were reported as bolder and feistier in their hazing of passers-by.

06/09/12: A purse that had been reported stolen after being accidently left in a Pizza Station restroom was discovered by staff in an adjoining restroom trash can. The employee who found the purse ran it down to the police department where it was reunited with its owner. Credit cards, a cell phone and ID were still in the purse, however approximately $120 in cash was reported missing.

06/11/12: Police contacted two very penitent individuals after catching them picking rhubarb stalks late night from the scenic garden at Sixth and Broadway Street.

06/14/12: Police were able to gain access into a vehicle in which the keys and a small child had been locked inside.

2012

06/15/12: Police received a marten live-trapped in town. Marten was transported out of town and released.

06/15/12: An officer was waved down by three German hikers at the Chilkoot trailhead in Dyea looking for a taxi back into Skagway. They had to turn back after they couldn't cross soft snow at the summit. All three ladies were loaded into the patrol car and given a lift back into town where the officer found them a camp spot for the night.

06/21/12: High winds were responsible for a large trampoline being blown over the fence from one backyard, taking out two telephone lines and landing against a neighboring vehicle.

06/23/12: A 32-year-old Skagway man was arrested and charged with second degree assault for stabbing a roommate with a kitchen butcher knife in a dispute over listening to country music in employee housing on Alaska Street. He was transported to Lemon Creek Correctional Center in Juneau. His 47-year-old victim was air medevaced to Bartlett Regional Hospital with serious stab wounds to his left arm.

06/24/12: Police responded to a report of a small vehicle stuck in the sand on the Dyea Flats. Officer was able to tow the vehicle to hard ground with his patrol car.

06/28/12: Police allowed a man to camp at Seven Pastures after he could not camp on the Dyea Flats as planned. The man's fifth wheel land yacht is 13' 6" wide, and the Tayia River Bridge is only 11' 2" wide.

06/29/12: Police gave a heavily intoxicated man, unable to walk, a ride home. After he was delivered by police, the man's employer called PD asking officers to give the man a ride elsewhere. Officers declined to furnish another ride.

06/30/12: Police spoke to campers at Seven Pastures about trash and beer cans all about.

06/30/12: Police received a traffic complaint about two vehicles racing about town. Both drivers were located, and told to return to Seven Pastures and stay off the city streets for the rest of the night.

06/30/12: A small black 4-wheeler trailer was reported abandoned in the front yard of a Broadway Street residence. The trailer has no license plate and the owner is unknown.

Best of the Skagway Police Blotter

07/01/12: Police intervened in what appeared to be a disturbance about to start on Fourth Avenue downtown. Officer instructed participants to pick up broken glass and be on their way.

07/01/12: Police investigated a report of an individual passed out in a downtown alleyway. They were able to waken the man and return him to family at Seven Pastures.

07/01/12: Police gave a half a dozen courtesy ride to individuals whom appeared too intoxicated to walk from downtown to Seven Pastures.

07/01/12: The grounds and restrooms at Seven Pastures were found to be heavily vandalized and trashed. Public Works reported the toilets had been torn out, and beer cans and human excrement was all over the grounds.

07/14/12: Police responded to a call of an unwanted couple at an Alaska Street residence. The couple, who had been fighting, left the residence and went their separate ways. The female half was contacted later after she advised she had nowhere but the street to spend the night. Police were able to borrow a tent from the residence she had been asked to vacate, and found another residence on State Street who took her in and allowed her to camp in their backyard for a couple of days until police were able to help her out of town on the ferry.

07/18/12: Police responded to a reported individual leaning against a residence where he did not belong on 19th Avenue. Police contacted the heavily intoxicated gentleman and convinced him he was not quite home yet.

07/19/12: Police located four unsecure businesses during a downtown security check. Police usually only find approximately four per week downtown.

07/19/12: Officer noticed a bicyclist weaving down 17th Avenue, however she fell off the bike before he could contact her. The officer gave the intoxicated cyclist a ride home.

07/20/12: Officer noticed a battered and bleeding man standing beside his bicycle near Seven Pastures. Individual declined medical attention, and the officer gave the intoxicated man and his bicycle a lift home.

07/21/12: A State Street resident delivered a bleeding intoxicated individual he found lying in the roadway near the Skagway River Bridge to the police department. An officer transported the man to the clinic where he was cleaned and stitched up. Afterwards, despite driving around town for 25 minutes the man was unable to remember where he lived. Police lodged the man in an open holding cell at the department for the night until he slept it off.

07/21/12: Police stopped to check the welfare of two individuals arguing on Fifth Avenue. Police gave a courtesy ride home to the female half. Too much alcohol consumption was apparently a factor.

07/21/12: Police cautioned two individuals against urinating downtown in public.

07/21/12: Police returned to an Alaska Street residence for a reported recurring disturbance. The male involved was told to leave the property lest he be arrested for trespass. Officers purchased a ferry ticket for the man to leave town. While waiting for the ferry, the man went to Pullen Creek Park where he passed out, prompting an aid call. Responding officers escorted him back to the ferry terminal, where he was refused passage due to his intoxicated condition.

07/22/12: Police received a report of an unconscious man on the sidewalk with his feet partially in the roadway on State Street. Officers were able to wake the man, and return him to a tent at Seven Pastures. Area was severely littered with beer cans and rubbish by visiting Haines softball team.

07/22/12: Police found a bicycle in the roadway on Main Street. Further investigation located a female with her pants down around her knees passed out under a tree. Officers were able to awaken her, re-dress her, and take her and her bicycle home.

07/22/12: An Alaska Street resident called to have an unwanted person removed from their property (again). The subject left on his own accord upon police arrival. Police had purchased a ferry ticket for the person earlier, however the ferry would not allow him to board due to his intoxicated condition. Subject advised he would be staying at a local motel for the night, and leave on the morning ferry.

07/23/12: A local resident complained of the trashing of the wooded area next to the ball fields after the softball tournament. His complaint was passed on to City Hall. The resident took it upon himself to clean the area.

07/23/12: Checking on why the subject who was supposed to leave town on the ferry never boarded, police were informed he was now working for the tribal council. Police cancelled the ticket.

Best of the Skagway Police Blotter

07/24/12: A woman stopped in to the police department to get directions back to her cruise ship. She was unable to comprehend the directions (alcohol consumption appeared to be a contributing factor) and she was given a ride back to her ship by an officer.

07/29/12: Police broke up a disturbance on Broadway Street between a girl, her friend, and a hero who tried to save her from him. Girlfriend and boyfriend sent on their ways, hero was transported to friend's house to sleep it off.

07/29/12: Caller reported an extremely intoxicated man apparently trying to open doors and windows at the bank. Subject urinated on back of building while caller was on phone to dispatch. Police located hero from the night before, who was once again transported to friend's house. Subject contacted police later that day as he needed help finding where he left his bike.

07/29/12: Police were able to gain access into a vehicle blocking the gas pumps with the keys locked inside.

08/02/12: Police contacted a family reportedly fighting on Broadway Street. Members were turned over to ship security, who

GARAGE GATEWAY – Brad Thoe, with wife Courtney and dachshund Dolly, stand outside their garage at the end of State Street. Brad had always admired AB Hall since he was a kid and wanted to build a shed or garage that resembled it. He used about 3,000 sticks collected from his work up the WP&YR tracks and co-worker Steve Burnham painted the Alaska flag. Also adorning the garage are a moose skull and antlers, two bulls (not native to this area), and a rare "Goarse" (inset). Brad claims that some horses were driven so hard during the gold rush that by the time they reached the summit, they grew goat horns.

were looking for the family due to earlier problems. After a shipboard meeting, the captain decided they were too much trouble and had them kicked off the ship.

08/03/12: Police were called to a Broadway Street residence on a call of an unknown man passed out on a bed inside the residence. Officer woke and escorted the man out. Subject was the same one police tried to get out of town on the ferry earlier.

08/08/12: Police assisted with the removal of an unwanted passenger from a train. The individual had told the train crew that he had a gun; turns out he did not.

08/08/12: Police assisted with the death investigation of a 70-year-old cruise ship passenger. The gentleman apparently died of natural causes.

08/09/12: Police received a report that a bucket half full of used motor oil was stolen from the bed of a pickup truck parked at the small boat harbor. Oil was said to have "no value."

08/10/12: Police assisted in rendering aid to, and then the death investigation of a 69-year-old Illinois man who apparently suffered a cardiac arrest while participating on a bicycle tour. EMS transported the man from the tour to the clinic, where he was pronounced dead by medical staff.

08/12/12: Police were asked to locate an extremely intoxicated individual last seen stumbling from downtown toward the ferry terminal. Police located the man, who was staying on a boat in the harbor. The officers decided the man was too intoxicated to stay aboard the boat by himself, and then spent about a half hour looking for a chaperone who could keep an eye on him for the rest of the night.

08/15/12: Police received a report from a cruise ship passenger who forgot her laptop in a downtown store that her laptop was now missing. Police reviewed the store security tape and believed they could locate the suspect, an apparent cruise ship member, shown taking the computer. Officers contacted the ships in port with a photo and description of the suspect. The next week a ship's captain returned the stolen laptop to the PD, who mailed it back to the victim.

08/16/12: Police investigated the reported theft of $1,000 cash from a motel room. Investigation stymied by premises suffering from a near total lack of key control or rudimentary security tools to limit possible suspects.

Best of the Skagway Police Blotter

08/17/12: Police responded to a loud disturbance in a downtown shop. The ruckus, in which items were knocked off the wall and on display and broken, was dismissed by the brawlers as a family argument. All parties declared the matter over, and agreed to go their separate ways.

08/17/12: Dispatch received a statewide attempt-to-locate on a vacationer missing somewhere in Alaska. Checking with U.S. Customs, it was discovered the man had hitchhiked into Skagway only a couple of hours prior. Police checked with food and lodging establishments in town, and was able to get word via an innkeeper to the man to call home.

08/18/12: Police gave a ride to a couple whose car broke down at U.S. Customs. The couple was transported to downtown where they picked up their trail permit from the Park Service, their train tickets from White Pass, and to the PD where they made arrangements to have car towed to Whitehorse for repairs. Police then transported them to Dyea where they were to hike the Chilkoot Trail the next day.

08/19/12: A wife notified police that her husband had been "goofing off" and got his truck stuck in the deep gravel on a highway emergency escape ramp. Dispatch located a piece of heavy equipment and an operator to remove the truck.

08/20/12: Police investigated a possible sexual assault occurring on a cruise ship. The victim reported to the investigating officer that she believed she had been touched inappropriately during a massage, even though she had gone back for massages twice since the alleged incident. After discussing her options she decided she did not want to pursue charges.

08/29/12: Police conducted a death investigation on a cruise ship passenger. Death of a 74-year-old Florida man was apparently from natural causes.

08/30/12: A wallet left behind by a passenger containing over $1,500 cash was turned over to police by a tour bus operator.

09/05/12: After a short foot pursuit, police contacted a reportedly intoxicated disgruntled patron from a downtown establishment. Patron was advised not to visit any more bars tonight, and to be nicer to bartenders once he did return.

09/09/12: Police investigated an explosion coming from employee housing at Fourth and State Street. A man who was burned after throwing gasoline on a bonfire was transported to the clinic by EMS. A

41-year-old Skagway man was arrested for disorderly conduct after he interfered with officers investigating the explosion. Same man arrested for assaulting his airport-wandering girlfriend earlier.

09/10/12: A jogger dropped a dog at the impound that had followed her all the way from Dyea Road. Police contacted the owner to come and get it. Shortly thereafter high school cross-country runners dropped off the same dog at the impound after it followed them from Dyea Road. Owner contacted again.

09/11/12: Police conducted a death investigation on a 79-year-old Vancouver, BC man. The cruise ship passenger appeared to have died of natural causes.

09/13/12: Police checked on a party at a State Street residence reportedly with underage drinkers in attendance. Officers failed to locate anybody under 21.

09/14/12: Dispatch took a cell phone call from a man who indicated he had been in a traffic accident somewhere over a cliff off Dyea Road. He said he was hurt and unable to get out of the vehicle. Police and EMS responded, and the man said he could hear the emergency vehicles and was eventually able to talk responders to the scene. A 28-year-old Skagway man was extracted and lifted up to the ambulance by rope rescue. He was transported to the clinic by EMS, and was subsequently cited for reckless driving by police.

09/14/12: A highly intoxicated State Street resident was escorted home after he was observed urinating in the middle of the intersection at Seventh and Broadway Street.

09/14/12: An Eighth Avenue resident reported she believed her pink wallet containing $500 was stolen at the same party the night before where underage drinking had been suspected.

09/15/12: Police and EMS responded to a reported unconscious and unresponsive male aboard the ferry Malaspina. The 69-year-old Juneau resident was transported to the clinic, where he was pronounced dead of apparent natural causes.

09/17/12: Police and Fire responded to a fire in a window box at a State Street residence. Box was torn away from the house and extinguished. The fire was possibly caused by errant cigarette being dropped in the box.

Best of the Skagway Police Blotter

09/19/12: Police and Fire responded to a fully involved tour bus fire on the Klondike Highway near Bridal Veil Falls. One passenger was transported to the clinic. Traffic on the highway was interrupted for about an hour.

09/19/12: A visitor center employee called to complain that employees with Klassique are outside enticing people to come in their store for end of season sales. She said she confronted the salesperson and told him that what he was doing was illegal, but he laughed her off when she told him that she will call the police. Dispatch told her that we were tied up on the fire call, to which the employee complained that there is "no police coverage on Broadway Street and everyone is doing whatever they want."

09/19/12: Police were called to a combative intoxicated man challenging people trying to cross the footbridge at the Dewey Lakes trailhead. The man refused to cooperate with the responding officer and came close to getting tasered before he was taken into protective custody and transported to a holding cell until he sobered up. This was the same man whom police tried to get to leave town with a free ferry ticket back in July.

09/26/12: A local resident brought to the PD some ID and photos of hiking equipment he found near Denver Glacier. Canadian paperwork found at the site indicates it may have been there since the early 1990s. Police were not able to locate any information on the owner.

10/14/12: Police responded to a reportedly intoxicated man who was without pants and had entered a Fifth Avenue residence by mistake. Officers transported him to Eighth Avenue where he belonged.

10/20/12: A 29-year-old Skagway man was cited for Reckless Driving after he left the scene of an early morning motor vehicle collision without reporting it. He allegedly drove his 1991 Ford Ranger pickup through a length of chain link fence surrounding TEMSCO property near the Ore Dock.

10/22/12: A wallet reported stolen from a party in mid-August was found by a hiker near Yakutania Point. The $500 said to be within the wallet at the time of the theft was no longer there.

10/23/12: Two brown bears were reported along the railroad tracks off Ninth Avenue.

10/27/12: Police cautioned waterfront and dock workers of a tsunami warning resulting from an earthquake off British Columbia. While there was no imminent danger they were advised not to turn their backs on the canal.

2012

10/29/12: Police received a complaint of suspicious firewood-taking near the Pioneer Cemetery.

10/29/12: Police received a call from a resident concerned for the safety of an individual kicking a flaming hacky sack near the Rec Center.

11/17 to 12/09/12: Police checked on and worked with responsible parties for numerous activated night watchmen lights in residences and businesses.

11/17 to 12/09/12: Police and Fire checked on and worked with responsible parties for numerous fire trouble alarms, mostly triggered by cold temperatures.

12/13/12: Police checked on a one car traffic accident on the Klondike Highway. The driver had buried his vehicle in a snow bank near the Moore Bridge. The rented U-Haul truck was pulled out of the bank by DOT; no damage to the vehicle or injury to the North Pole driver.

12/18/12: Police checked on a downtown door blown open by wind and snow. Responsible party contacted.

12/19/12: Police returned a wooden bench that had blown into the street to the boardwalk.

12/23/12: Police checked and secured an unoccupied residence on 18th Avenue at which the front door had blown open.

12/29/12: Caretaker of a Broadway Street business told police that he believed that someone had entered the business and maliciously turned the furnace off at the breaker box, causing the building to freeze and the pipes to burst.

12/29/12: North end residents reported hearing several loud booms. Police believe they located the party from where the sounds were originating, however it appeared over and participants were heading home.

SEEN ON THE WIND

Movie star/pilot Harrison Ford does a pre-flight check of his private plane on the tarmac before leaving the Skagway airport. Ford and girl friend Calista Flockhart and her son Liam took a train ride and overnighted at the White House B&B while stopping here on a trip to Alaska in July 2008. Left, TV and film star Flockhart kisses Ford before she climbs on his plane with Liam. – *Molly Dischner*

Heard on the Wind

Even more perplexing missives from our fabulous visitors

A passenger off the Mercury who was in his 80s complained to a SMART bus driver that there were too many 90-year-olds on the boat. – 05/15/09

A lady came into the visitor center and wanted to know if the 1906 photo of the school in the lobby was real, and if the kids in the photo were real. Another person comes into the visitor center, looks up at the ceiling, and asks: "Is this building is still standing?" – 05/15/09

A woman off a ship asked where she could buy perfume in Skagway. The windy one was stumped. In 33 years, we have been asked all sorts of questions, but never that one. A couple other business owners were on the dock; neither had a clue as to where perfume could be purchased. One sniffed her pits, and the windy one told the woman that he preferred "Wood Smoke Enchantment." The woman said she would try Ketchikan or Juneau. – 05/29/09

A woman came up to a local and asked, "What do you call these boardwalks?" The local said, "Boardwalks." – 06/12/09

Four tourists photographed the old Kirmse's and Moe's signs on the rocks above town. Then, as they turned to go, one woman remarked, "Well, I think it must be phony because there wouldn't be any way to get up there." – 06/12/09

Overheard by the big rhubarb plant at Fifth and Broadway:
"This is old growth rhubarb?"
"This is rhubarb on steroids."
"Is that celery? Lettuce?"
"They feed this rhubarb moose poop?" – 06/26/09

HEARD ON THE WIND

Gunnalcheesh for this one...

A man with seeming intelligence asked a local resident, "What's the Native language around here?" When told it was Tlingit, the visitor stated, "That's funny – I'd have thought it was Indian."

– 06/29/06

WINDY NIGHT INDEED – The Skagway string band "Windy Valley Boys" performs their usual Monday night set at the Red Onion Saloon.

– Katie Emmets

A visitor at the VC asked if the "clock on the hillside works?"

Answer, "Absolutely, twice a day." – 07/10/09

A visitor approached the windy one, who was handing out papers with the newsies on the dock.

"Where is my tour?" the visitor asked.

"I don't know," said the windy one, who is always happy to assist. "Do you have a ticket I can see?"

"No!" she said, and stormed off. – 07/10/09

A man was looking over a sale flyer at an outdoor store and saw a featured discount on bear spray. He looked confused and said, "Bear spray? So is that like some perfume or cologne you wear that bears don't like? I just don't see how that could work!!!" – 07/10/09

"I'm looking for the calving tour?"
"Calving what?"
"Glaciers, of course" – 07/24/09

"Where is the McDonald's in town?"
"Sorry, we have no restaurant chains here," replied a local store clerk, but the tourist was perplexed.
"Do you SEE any golden arches?" responded the local. – 07/24/09

HEARD ON THE WIND

On an overcast morning on Broadway, a tourist admired the floral display in front of a store. "Wow, look how beautiful those flowers are. I wonder how they do that with no sunshine." – 07/24/09

A visitor on the dock complained about how long the walk was to the train (maybe 100 yards). The conductor gave his usual explanation that Alaska is a big state. The visitor replied that he was from Texas. The conductor replied that Alaska was three times the size of Texas. The visitor walked away toward the train in a huff. – 07/24/09

A visitor asked two newsie boys if they were brothers. In unison, one answered, "Yes" and the other answered "No." The visitor still took a paper, but the boys missed a tip. – 07/24/09

One tourist said to another on Broadway, "I've never seen this many tourists in one place. I wonder how they all get here?" – 08/28/09

A wise guy pointed to the subhead on the front of the Skaguay Alaskan visitor guide, "1,000 Miles North of Worry", and asked, "Where is Worry? I've never heard of a community named Worry."
The windy one laughed and congratulated the man on stumping the editor. Further research has revealed there is a Worry, North Carolina, located in Burke County, about 25 miles from where the editor grew up. The headline will not be corrected, as we are still about 1,000 miles north of the collective Worry (aka Canada's lower provinces and our own Lower 48 states), where people hurry about for no apparent reason. The slogan "1,000 Miles North of Worry" came from a Skagway Chamber of Commerce brochure around the time of statehood (circa 1959).

And speaking of Soapy, a man on the Railroad Dock asked the windy one about the skull on the rocks, saying it was great art. He was told it was "Soapy Smith's Skull" and painted some time after the desperado's violent demise in 1898.
The inquirer seemed disappointed.
"I'm a big Grateful Dead fan," he said. "I thought it might be a Dead skull."
"Sorry, it ain't Jerry (Garcia), man," replied the windy one. "But if it helps, our Soapy can sing a mean 'Friend of the Devil.'"
That one was for Jim "Soapy" Richards. You have been a great ambassador for Skagway since the mid-1970s (when we had five ships a week). The News gang wishes you all the best in your retirement from the Broadway stage after 35 years, a truly amazing run. If you get a chance, catch his last show at the Eagles Hall at 2:30 p.m. on Thursday, Sept. 17th and send him off in style. The News will be there for sure. We love you more than Jerry, man. Good health to you and Terri. Mahalo – 09/11/09

HEARD ON THE WIND

A visitor came in to ask about Termination Dust. "Is that what makes the glaciers dirty?" – 09/25/09

A tour salesman standing in front of the Golden North was asked by a tourist, who pointed at the electrical lines coming down from Lower Lake, "Is that the zip line?" – 05/14/10

"I was talking to a lady from southern Mississippi today and asked her how they were dealing with the oil spill on the Gulf Coast. After explaining how devastating it will be to the fisheries, economy, etc., she asked me, 'Well how did y'all recover after your Juan Valdez oil spill?'

"Didn't really know what to say…maybe should've come back with 'We're still cleaning up the coffee grounds.'" – 05/28/10

A customer in a store with a coupon book very seriously approached a salesperson with a free coupon and remarked, "You aren't fooling people, we know you only do this to get us into your store, so we'll spend some money!" – 06/11/10

A large woman came into a store huffing and puffing. "It must be the altitude," she said.
After being informed Skagway was at sea level, she tried to make up another excuse. – 06/11/10

Questions heard but unanswered on the last no-ship Sunday:
"What time is the northern lights showing?"
"Do you have jackalopes up here?"
"Is the snow real, or do you spray it up there for the tourists?"
"How did they paint that building (AB Hall) to make it look like that?" – 06/11/10

A woman holds up a Canadian dollar in a store and asks, "This is your money, right?"
"No, ma'am, that's Canadian."
Clearly flustered, she huffs, "Well then what kind of money do you take?"
"American, ma'am."
Confused, she stammers, "What? Why?"
"Because this is America."
"Well, I'm from New Jersey, and we don't have Canadian money there."
Trying to be as cordial as possible, the clerk responded, "Nor do we have it here ma'am. I need you to pay in American dollars or with a credit card."
Almost desperately, the woman says, "But I don't know where I got this money – someone on this trip must have given it to me!"

HEARD ON THE WIND

"Were you in Vancouver?"
"Yes... but they don't use Canadian there." – 07/09/10

A tour driver pulled off the road at a photo stop on the pass after crossing the border into Canada. Everyone got out except a young woman and her father.
She said to him, "Here, I thought Alaska was an island. Now I find out it's part of Canada!"
– 07/09/10

"Is this water out here man-made?"
"Why are there so many Alaska license plates here?" – 07/09/10

A woman is sitting outside and asks the difference between Alaska and the Yukon Territory.
A local replies, "Alaska is in the U.S. and the Yukon is part of Canada."
"Oh, ok," she says, "so where are we then?" – 07/23/10

While standing on the dock in his Mountie costume picking up passengers for a train tour, a guide was approached by a visitor, who said, "You're not a real Mountie. You're in America." – 07/23/10

A man came into a store, looked at a picture of puffins, and asked the clerk, "Why do Alaskans hate puffins so much?"
After scratching her head, the clerk said, "Huh?"
"There are signs everywhere," he said.
After another puzzled look from the clerk, the man continued, "The puffin with the red circle around him."
The clerk explained it was a no smoking sign. – 07/23/10

A local was down in the harbor parking lot the other day, noticing how low the tide was. She looked up and saw a tourist standing there looking at her, and remarked, "Wow, this is an extremely low tide. I don't think I've noticed a low tide like this before."
The visitor replied, "I was thinking the same thing. Have you not had much rain lately?" – 07/23/10

"Where do they get the name, Skagway?" a visitor asks.
The guide proceeds to explain the Tlingit meaning of the word.
"Oh, okay, because people say, 'You old skag, and that's not a nice thing to say to somebody."
– 07/23/10

"So what is there to do in Skagway?"

"Well the salmon derby is going on right now."

"How do they train the salmon to race?" – 07/23/10

A guy comes into the rock shop ooohing and aaahing at all the rocks saying what a great place this is for rocks. The owner told him it is. Then he says it must be a real haven in this area for a gynecologist. At the same shop, a female tourist inquired about how to care for the semi-fragile rock she was considering. Off the top of her head, the storekeeper suggested she not drop it. "I mean how do you bathe it?" she asked. The shopkeeper was dumbfounded. After sharing this story with another local, it was suggested that she should have told her to use "soapstone." – 08/13/10

A woman comes into the visitor center and asks, "How old is this building?"

"About 110 years!"

"Oh," she said, " I can't believe it's still alive!"

A man looking at the AB Hall then asks: "Is the front of the building made out of antlers?" – 08/13/10

A lady came up to the train station window and said, "We want to go to the summit".

The agent said, "OK".

She then asks the price and when told it's $115, she goes "Whaaaaaat?! I heard it was $4."

The agent kindly tells her no, that it was in fact $115.

She then said, "So when you get to the summit you can see Russia right?"

The agent laughed but said nothing.

The visitor then said, "That's a joke in the United States." – 08/13/10

A man came into the visitor center and asked how tall the mountains are around town. He was told approximately 5,000 feet.

"That can't be," the man responded. "The train only goes to 2,000 feet. – 08/13/10

One couple riding the train asked, "How often do the rangers build the glaciers?" – 08/13/10

A Haines man called to file a "complaint" about Skagway. A friend was getting married and a bachelor party was being organized. So he calls the Red Onion Saloon asking if any of the brothel girls would be willing to come over to Haines and be a stripper for $250. There were no takers. "Your prostitutes aren't real," he complained. – 08/27/10

HEARD ON THE WIND

A woman walks into the visitors center and says, "A friend of mine came last month and she was sitting in front of this building and saw people taking pictures and couldn't figure out what they were taking pictures of. Then she realized it was all wood. So I came in to find out what she didn't know."

– 08/27/10

A local man parked in front of the hardware store with his dog in the back of his truck. A visitor asked, "Why do all the guys in Alaska have dogs in the back of their truck?"

The local replied, "Because the women insist on riding in the front." – 08/27/10

At the overlook, a bus passenger was admiring the costumes worn by the streetcar drivers. Curious, she asked one of them, "Do you have any male drivers?"

And the streetcar driver replied, "No everybody goes right to the post office." – 08/27/10

IDIOT WIND – The above photo submitted by Greg Jones needs no explanation. Don't do this, ever! – *Greg Jones*

"I really hate when they stand in the middle of the road taking pictures or just walking down the street oblivious to vehicular traffic around them," said one man.

The man with him agreed, as they both walked down the middle of Broadway with a truck and bus behind them. – 09/10/10

A customer came up and asked, "In your bulk taffy bin, do you have salmonberry flavor in it?"

The employee replied, "No, we sell the salmonberry taffy separate in its own bag."

"Oh good, because I'm allergic to fish and I just wanted to make sure before I bought from the bulk taffy bin." – 09/10/10

117

HEARD ON THE WIND

As a people-mover was driving her cart back to the ship on the Railroad Dock's aft berth, and weaving around tourists, the little old lady sitting next to the driver remarked, "It looks like a damn Wal-Mart parking lot." – 09/10/10

A man coming out of the Red Onion commented to his wife, "It's better than Hooters!" – 09/24/10

Where do they (Skagwegians) put all the wildlife in the winter time?" – 09/24/10

The first breath of wind has arrived ahead of the first ship. A former resident was heading up to Skagway this spring to see friends and told his young daughter that he was going to Alaska. She then asked, "Do they speak English in Alaska?" – 04/29/11

A dog musher pulled up to the post office. A visitor looked at the box of the truck with the dog windows in the back, and asked, "Is that the dog catcher?" 05/27/11

A local 10-year-old girl selling lemonade was asked if she was Sarah Palin's daughter. – 06/10/11

A visitor came in and announced he did not want a tour, he just wanted to do what the locals did. He was offered a job, but declined. – 06/10/11

A local woman was sitting at the Station in her Red Sox hat. A man she has never seen before walks by with a Yankees hat. The usual banter ensues. The Yankee fan proceeds to say, "but I'm actually from New York. You aren't from Boston. You're in Alaska."
She informed him that he too was in Alaska, to which he had no response. – 06/10/11

After a bus driver stopped on the Klondike to let his riders look at a bear on the side of the road, one woman got up and tried to get out the door.
The driver would not let her out, but the woman kept trying, so the driver got up and blocked her from the doorway.
The woman was told bears can be dangerous. She then asked why the tour drivers don't tranquilize them so people like her can go up and pet them. –06/24/11

"What's the altitude/elevation here?"
"Well, we're at sea level here in town."

HEARD ON THE WIND

"Yeah, but sea level here isn't the same as sea level where I'm from." – 06/24/11

A tourist walks up to the railroad ticket counter: "I just read in the bathroom that this is the most scenic railroad in the world."
Agent: "Well, in my experience, bathroom walls are never wrong." – 06/24/11

While standing in front of the AB Hall, one woman says to the other, "Look, it is just a bunch of sticks." The other woman replies, "that's because that was all there was to build with." – 07/15/11

"We're just a couple of weeks early. They bring in the grizzlies when the salmon start to run."
– 07/15/11

A woman came into the visitor center to ask where she could catch a bus to the city.
"You are in the city."
"Where is the bus out of the city?" – 07/29/11

A local's daughter was visiting Skagway on a break from college. The local and her daughter were making plans to visit Laughton Glacier the following day. The local mentioned to her daughter that they would bring bear spray to Laughton Glacier as there had been reports of a lot of bear activity on the trail. The daughter thoughtfully absorbed this information without comment.
The following morning as they were getting their gear together to head to the train station the daughter said to her mother, "Shall I spray the bear repellent on now, or wait until we get to the trailhead?"
– 07/29/11

Sitting near the footbridge at Dyea watching the salmon and waiting patiently for the grizzly to show up, a local was asked by a passing tourist, "Why do they call it the salmon run when the salmon can't really run?" – 08/12/11

Asked of the staff at the visitor center: "Are your bathrooms for people?" – 08/12/11

A SMART bus driving into town from the Railroad Dock is stopped at the tracks by a train. While waiting for the train to pass, two ladies sitting behind the shuttle driver are talking.
One asks, "I wonder what that is," pointing to the fish weir.
The second woman, without pause, says "Oh, that's a safety net so you can go swimming and not worry about the bears getting you." –08/26/11

HEARD ON THE WIND

A man came in to ask about his ancestor who may have died in Skagway. The visitor center staff said they would be happy to try to find any information. However, when asked for the goldrusher's name, the man said he wasn't sure, he would have to go look it up. – 08/26/11

A visitor observing the salmon in Pullen Creek asked, "Why are you letting all the fish die?"
– 08/26/11

"Is Skagway in the United States part of Alaska, or the British Columbia part of Alaska?" – 09/09/11

"How many more (towns) until we reach Alaska?" – 09/09/11

A woman who worked a summer here in 1999 asked, "Is the waterfall by the cemetery still there?"
– 09/09/11

"What do you think of the girls dressed up in the Red Onion? All those bosoms must get the seniors very excited!" – 09/09/11

A woman asked where everyone in Skagway lived. She was told there are 20-plus blocks of houses here.
"No, there aren't any houses. Where does everyone live?"
She continued to insist there were no houses regardless of what she was told. – 09/09/11

Another driver who took a group up the White Pass into Canada was asked if they were going to Russia, or if they could "see Russia from the top of the pass." – 09/09/11

On a rare sunny day in August, a visitor came in and grumbled, "Why would a cruise ship come here?"
The clerk felt like throttling him, but held her tongue.
A few minutes later, another man came in and said, "This is my favorite of the three places we have been."
Life was good again. – 09/09/11

From the shelter of the tour shack...
"Do the whales come out in the rain?"
"How much is the $2.00 tour?" – 09/09/11

2013

Winter vehicle trackdowns, ferry ticket dude at it again, smelly salmon reports, and hooked-up couples in various stages of street mischief.

01/01/13: Police received a 911 call from an intoxicated Alaska Street resident who just wanted someone to talk to. Police checked on the residence.

01/29/13: Police searched for a truck driver reportedly stuck in the snow at MP 10 on the Klondike Highway. Driver saved by Good Samaritan, highway closed for the night.

01/29/13: An officer stopped a vehicle driven by a 41-year-old Skagway man for failing to stop at a stop sign. The driver appeared intoxicated, and failing field tests was transported to the police station where he blew a .35 BAC. He was charged with driving under the influence of intoxicants and given a ride home.

02/09/13: Police responded to a call of an unwanted patron causing a disturbance at a downtown establishment. Police took the highly intoxicated man back to his motel room and told him he would have to stay put for the night, and not return to the business. Police re-contacted the man moments later shuffling down the street back to the bar. Police picked him up and transported him to a holding cell where he spent the night.

02/20/13: Police were called to a domestic disturbance. The officer attempted to give the male half a ride to a motel to spend the night. However once at the motel the 38-year-old Skagway man, the same one police tried to buy a ferry ticket for last year, wanted to fight with the officer. He was jailed and charged with disorderly conduct.

Best of the Skagway Police Blotter

03/02/13: Responding to three 911 reports of a loud crash, police investigated a traffic collision in which a vehicle pushed a parked utility trailer up onto the sidewalk, as well as striking part of a building. The vehicle was gone on arrival, however the officer was able to follow a groove cut into State Street by the vehicle being driving on a rim only after the tire was torn off. The groove led to a residence on 22nd Avenue, where police located a 20-year-old Skagway woman hiding in a back bathroom. She was charged with minor consuming alcohol, negligent driving and leaving the scene of an accident.

03/11/13: Police received a report of a noisy disturbance in the street at Fourth and Main. Tracks in snow indicate two individuals left a tavern at that address and danced or wrestled in the street. Parties then left the area, where one set of tracks wandered to a basement apartment at Seventh and Main Street, and the other to an alley apartment behind Ninth and Spring Street. Both residences were quiet upon police arrival.

03/14/13: Police sealed for Alaska Fish and Game three locally trapped wolverine, one locally trapped wolf, and ten locally trapped marten hides.

03/18/13: Police checked on a dead moose in the trees along the rifle range road. Moose appears to have expired from natural causes.

03/23/13: Police stopped a vehicle for speeding on Main Street. The driver, a 45-year-old Wasilla man, appeared intoxicated and after failing field tests was arrested for DUI. He was transported to the police department where he blew a .185 BAC. While officers completed the paperwork to release him on his own recognizance, he became combative and smashed a telephone and digital recorder. The seasonal construction worker was housed in a holding cell and additionally charged with criminal mischief and resisting arrest.

03/24/13: Police investigated a late night traffic collision that took out a 30-foot section of fence and destroyed three telephone booths on State Street. Using a license plate left behind at the scene, an officer was able to track the wreckage to an extensively damaged pickup and a 42-year-old Wasilla man, who was subsequently charged with leaving the scene of an accident and negligent driving.

03/26/13: Police checked on a tug boat stranded on the rocks in the small boat harbor.

04/06/13: Police issued a verbal warning for speed to a departing city manager trying to leave town.

04/19/13: Responding to a disturbance, police found an uncooperative intoxicated man (ferry ticket dude) in a blood-strewn apartment. Police were unable to find other participants or victims. He refused medical treatment to his injured hand. Police warned the man that while it was legal to bleed all over his residence, it was not legal to disturb neighbors while doing so.

04/23/13: Police searched for a vehicle reported stolen from a Second Avenue residence. Vehicle was located at Fairway Market – owner had walked home after shopping and had forgotten the vehicle was in the parking lot.

04/26/13: Police checked on apparent soap bubbles foaming out of a manhole cover on State Street.

EAGLES AT PLAY – Top, members of the Fraternal Order of Eagles celebrate during a veterans-themed state convention held in Skagway in 2012, while a trio of bald eagles defend their salmon catch from pesky crows on a sandbar in the Taiya River in Dyea in 2013.

Best of the Skagway Police Blotter

04/27/13: Police picked up a highly intoxicated individual passed out and lying on Seventh Avenue. Individual threw up repeatedly in patrol car while being driven home to residence on 20th Avenue.

04/27/13: Police requested an amorous, intoxicated couple to cease and desist from having sex against the outer wall of a State Street business.

04/28/13: Police checked two large pallet fires at Mountain View campground. Groups of Canadians who were trapped in town due to a landslide-caused road closure were trying to stay warm in freezing weather. All available rooms in town were taken. They were asked to please keep fires and noise down to a minimum. The officer also asked a man who was juggling two kerosene-soaked fire torches in the campground to cease and desist.

05/06/13: Police were called to a reported assault at employee housing at Fourth and Spring Street. The responding officer found a 37-year old Skagway man on the ground, being held down by four other men. One had a bleeding lip and said the man had assaulted him, and the other men said they had witnessed the assault. The man refused to cooperate with the officer and get into the patrol car and needed assistance from a shock from the officer's taser. He was arrested and charged with domestic violence assault.

05/17/13: Police checked on a large illegal, unpermitted burn at approximately 2.5 mile Klondike Highway. Responsible party refused to put the fire out and at one point the intoxicated landowner appeared and ordered fire and police personnel off the property. The Fire Department spent almost two hours extinguishing the blaze; charges of illegal burning and burning hazardous materials are pending against the property owner.

05/19/13: A man reported his life had been threatened and he needed help immediately before hanging up. Police responded and found a bad combination of too much alcohol and too much bear spray. Parties separated and agreed to stay away from each other.

05/21/13: Police responded to a shoplift complaint. Suspect crew member was returned to the cruise ship's security personnel and asked not that he not be allowed to disembark in Skagway anymore.

05/22/13: Police and Fire responded to a fire at the Skagway Fish Company on Congress Way. Kitchen area of restaurant was fully engulfed; kitchen and restaurant portions were a total loss due to smoke or fire damage. Police suspect arson by a former employee.

05/22/13: A possible pet bunny wearing a collar was reported loose and being pestered by a crow near Fourth and State Street.

05/22/13: A visitor called 911 requesting officer assistance. He reported that his wife had too much to drink, is not listening to him and was walking away.

05/22/13: Caller reported that she was forced to take refuge in the bathroom while her roommate was pounding on door attempting to gain entry. Our 39-year-old ferry ticket dude was arrested for domestic violence assault and taken into custody despite his best efforts to resist arrest.

05/24/13: Police and EMS responded to a brawl involving a large number of patrons at the Bonanza. One assault victim was transported to the clinic with a possible broken jaw and concussion. Police stopped one group of a dozen locals pursuing a half dozen Canadians into Pullen Park and the small boat harbor. EMS reported another group was leaving their friend at the clinic and advised they were going to "take matters into their own hands." Police spent the night keeping the groups separated, and after investigating found nothing criminal besides mutual combat. Both groups said they planned to go to Haines on the afternoon ferry. Haines PD was given a heads up.

05/25/13: Police were called to Mountain View RV Park on a complaint of an intoxicated man breaking windows on an RV. Police responded and the victim pointed out the bloody smashed window, and the intoxicated man lying under a nearby tree. The Skagway ferry ticket dude, 39, was arrested for criminal mischief (breaking windows on an RV) and violating previous conditions of release. Magistrate ordered him held on bail; he was later transported to Lemon Creek prison in Juneau.

05/25/13: A 29-year-old seasonal employee was arrested for domestic violence assault. The man allegedly choked and badly burned his girlfriend on a bedroom heater. Magistrate ordered him held on bail; he was later transported to Lemon Creek prison in Juneau.

05/29/13: Ketchikan police called requesting assistance in recovering $24,000 worth of jewelry stolen from a Ketchikan jewelry store. Suspects were identified as passengers aboard the Norwegian Jewel. Ship security put a responding officer in touch with the suspects, and the jewelry was recovered from their stateroom safe. The suspects, an elderly Iowa couple were removed from the ship by the captain, and they were in turn escorted to the airport and out of Skagway by police.

Best of the Skagway Police Blotter

05/29/13: An officer stopped a vehicle for speeding on Main Street. During this traffic stop the officer was contacted by a bicyclist who wanted to know why the officer was hassling the motorist. The bicyclist refused to move on as requested by the officer. Once the motorist was released with a warning, the officer directed his attention to the confrontational bicyclist. While talking, the officer discovered the man was armed with a loaded .40 pistol. The 21-year-old Idaho man was charged with misconduct with a weapon for failing to disclose he had a concealed handgun on his person.

06/01/13: Police interviewed the Fish Company arson suspect at length. Suspect demanded a lie detector test, and when he understood the department could offer one he fled town for Washington state the next morning. Police will be seeking a warrant for his return.

06/02/13: Hikers found a 53-year-old man lying on the ground after suffering a 15-20 foot fall near Smuggler's Cove. The man, who reportedly had been lying there for over an hour, may have a broken hip. EMS recovered the man and transported him to the clinic.

06/03/13: A 35-year-old Juneau man was held overnight after police determined he could not care for himself. The intoxicated man had been banned from each drinking establishment in town and fought with officers after refusing to quiet down and go to his hotel room to sleep it off. Officers had to fight him into the patrol car, fight him out of the patrol car and fight him into the holding cell, where he continued to beat and bang and kick the door and yell threats for the next hour.

06/09/13: A passenger reported to police that a whale bone carving and some clothing were stolen from her luggage on the state ferry between Juneau and Skagway.

06/11/13: Police conducted a death investigation aboard the Sapphire Princess. Passenger apparently expired from natural causes, and the body remained aboard for Juneau.

06/13/13: Police responded to a reported overturned toy raft floating down the swollen Taiya River. Three intoxicated men and a large black lab made it to shore safely and were able to call from a cabin.

06/14/13: Dispatch received a complaint from a visitor that clothing sold in town was advertised to have been made in Italy, when in actuality it was made in Turkey. She was concerned that such fraud looked poorly upon Skagway.

06/16/13: Police responded to a fight between intoxicated Haines and Whitehorse residents that spilled out onto the street from inside the Bonanza. Parties were separated and monitored throughout the morning for additional flare-ups.

06/16/13: Additional contacts were made with the above for drinking in a city park, disturbing the peace and urinating and defecating in public.

06/16/13: While dealing with the above, police stopped a speeding vehicle. A 36-year-old Skagway man was cited for driving on a revoked driver's license and warned about driving while intoxicated. Officers told him he was lucky they were too busy to process him for DUI, however they seized his keys for the night.

06/17/13: Officers responded to a disturbance at a Broadway Street residence. An intoxicated male was arguing and shoving his roommates. He agreed to spend the night elsewhere.

06/20/13: Police responded to a neighbor vs. neighbor dispute on 20th Avenue where one man resorted to pulling a gun on the other. All involved decided the situation should never have gotten out of hand and the neighbors agreed to co-exist peacefully.

06/20/13: A local person out for a walk was reportedly told by a dock worker that he was a "customs agent" and he would arrest her for watching the ships arrive if she did not leave the area.

06/23/13: Police offered a ride home to an individual exhibiting wise judgment by sleeping on the ground under his vehicle rather than driving home intoxicated from the solstice party. Man declined the ride, advising he was happy where he was.

06/27/13: Police gave a heavily intoxicated Haines man a ride to the small boat harbor; man had reported he was unable to find his fishing boat and was afraid he had been left in Skagway.

06/29/13: Police asked campers at Seven Pastures to clean up empty beer cans and other garbage left strewn around.

06/30/13: Officers responded to a late night fight at Seven Pastures.

06/30/13: Police stopped a vehicle for driving without headlights. Driver was unable to locate headlight switch. Keys were taken from driver who agreed to walk home and return when sober.

Best of the Skagway Police Blotter

SKAGWAY WEDDING DAY – Weddings in the Skagway magistrate's office at City Hall are common in the summer, but the above couple went all out with a fancy wedding dress and a professional photo shoot on the municipal government steps and lawn. – *Katie Emmets*

06/30/13: Two Whitehorse residents were held overnight for safekeeping after it was determined they were unable to care for themselves. Both were discovered lying on Main Street after trying to drag an ice chest behind two stolen bicycles. One registered bicycle was returned to the local owner. One 20-year-old was cited for minor in possession of alcohol.

07/03/13: Police responded to a downtown establishment after receiving a complaint of a disturbance. A bartender had a highly intoxicated combative man restrained after he pushed other patrons. Police arrested a 26 year old Mt. Vernon, WA man who also attempted to flee from the patrol car once parked at the police department and had to tackled and carried into the building. He was charged with trespass and attempted escape.

07/04/13: Police stopped a vehicle for erratic driving. After failing field tests a 22-year-old Skagway man was arrested for DUI and transported to the police station where he blew a .24 BAC. He was cited and was released on his promise to appear in court.

2013

07/04/13: Police were able to open a vehicle in which a dog had locked the passengers out.

07/04/13: Police contacted and warned five highly intoxicated people committing criminal mischief (flipping shopping carts and picnic tables) on Fourth Avenue.

07/05/13: Police investigated a non-injury one-car traffic collision near Long Bay. A 35-year-old Skagway man was arrested for DUI and transported to the police station where he blew a .24 BAC. As the man had two prior DUI convictions, he was held over for court.

07/05/13: Police warned a highly intoxicated individual about stealing a bicycle from a downtown establishment. Police found the man in the roadway after he fell off the bicycle less than a block from where he took it.

07/08/13: Police arrested a one-legged man in a wheel chair who apparently rode the state ferry Columbia from Bellingham to Skagway without purchasing a ticket or possessing a boarding pass, personal identification or money. The 24-year-old Las Vegas man was booked on theft of services charges.

07/12/13: Police responded to an Alaska Street residence reporting that a young woman who did not live there had attempted to gain entry. Police later found a highly intoxicated woman passed out on a sidewalk on State Street. Police were able to wake the woman, and gave her a ride to her cabin.

07/14/13: Police awoke a highly intoxicated man in the Pullen Creek park shelter and told him he could not drink the rest of his beverages in the park.

07/15/13: Police are investigating a shattered window and assault at the Bonanza in which one intoxicated patron shoved a second intoxicated patron against said window, reportedly over the attention of a female.

07/16/13: Police and Public Works responded to a reported "awful smell" on Broadway Street. Smell was determined to have come from a Dumpster that contained fish carcasses.

07/17/13: Fire officials discovered a campfire outside the fire ring at Smuggler's Cove. Fire asked police to respond to ask the hot dog cookers to extinguish the illegal burn, and to use the provided fire pit.

Best of the Skagway Police Blotter

07/17/13: Police responded to reported sparring spouses at a downtown business. Police gave a courtesy ride home to the female half.

07/18/13: Police are investigating the possible theft of a $5,000 commercial freezer from one business by another business.

07/19/13: White Pass reported that two bicycles left on the tracks near the shops had been run over by a train, and were "pretty mangled."

07/20/13: Police transported an unwanted patron home from a Broadway Street bar. Officers helped him crawl through a bedroom window after it was discovered he had locked himself out of the house.

07/20/13: Police and EMS responded to the small boat harbor for two individuals injured by rough waters on two separate boats. Patients suffering a knee and a back injury were transported to the clinic.

07/20/13: Police and Fire responded to a fire at Hidden Cove. High winds were pushing the ground fire through the peat and woody soil. Police also confiscated a large tent illegally set up in the area.

07/21/13: Two patrons of a downtown establishment walked into the alley and into the headlights of a patrol car that happened to be parked there. Apparently not noticing the headlights, the men started to urinate against the outside of the bar. Police then shown a spotlight onto the men. The men walked out of the spotlight, and walked behind a neighboring building continuing their business. Police then contacted them and tried to make it clear that the men should have instead used the facilities inside the bar.

07/24/13: A passerby passed on to police a found wallet containing almost $500 in cash. Dispatch was able to locate the owner and return the wallet.

07/27/13: After receiving multiple inquiries and complaints about explosions on the north end of town, an employee party on the Klondike Highway was asked to cease and desist.

07/28/13: Police stopped a vehicle for failing to stop at a stop sign and erratic driving on Main Street. The driver appeared intoxicated, and failed field sobriety tests. A 31-year-old Skagway man was arrested for DUI and transported to the police station where he blew a .20 BAC. He was cited and released.

2013

07/28/13: A man wanted dispatch to know that he had lost his raft and ended up in the river, but was safe and sound in case somebody spotted the empty raft.

07/29/13: Police stopped a vehicle for no tail lights while driving on Main Street. The driver appeared intoxicated and failed field sobriety tests. A 39-year-old Skagway man was arrested for DUI and transported to the police station where he refused to submit to a breath test. He was cited for DUI and refusal to submit to chemical test and released on his promise to appear.

07/30/13: EMS and police responded to a down bicyclist near the Moore Creek Bridge. Patient was transported to the clinic, and later to a Coast Guard helicopter for a medevac.

08/01/13: Police responded to a reported passenger vs. crewmember assault onboard the ferry Matanuska. A Pennsylvania man was briefly held in custody at the PD during the investigation.

08/02/13: Dispatch received a myriad of calls from annoyed residents inquiring about a stuck cruise ship horn.

08/02/13: A gentleman approached and asked dispatch if we had a report of a missing driver's license he had found. Dispatch difficultly pried from the man that he had found a small purse containing many credit cards, ID, and the license. Dispatched told the man that we handle many such items, almost every day. Man didn't trust that dispatch could/would track down the owner and return the items, and was sure it would be better if he mailed the items back to the owner himself.

08/03/13: Police stopped a vehicle for failing to stop at a stop sign and erratic driving on Main Street. The driver appeared intoxicated and failed field sobriety tests. A 22-year-old Whitehorse man was arrested and charged with DUI and refusal to submit to chemical test. He was held for three days awaiting a hearing after being unable to raise $1,000 bail.

08/03/13: A report that two dogs were left inside a vehicle with no ventilation reached police. The reporting party was able to find the owners in a restaurant, however they seemed unconcerned even though they agreed to roll down a window. Reporting party was concerned they may try to park the car elsewhere and try it again.

08/04/13: Police received a complaint of eight or nine poorly filleted salmon dumped in the river near Seven Pastures. The complainant was concerned the carcasses were a nuisance and a bear attractant.

131

Best of the Skagway Police Blotter

All week: Police responded to dozens of calls of people molesting salmon and suspected fishing without a license in Pullen Creek/Pond.

08/07/13: Police warned an argumentative and uncooperative bicycle rider who could not fathom that he was not allowed to ride after dark without lights while carrying a second individual on his handlebars.

08/08/13: Police told a couple lying in the middle of Broadway Street that it was dangerous to do so. Couple said they had been looking at the stars.

08/10/13: A 27-year-old seasonal employee from New Jersey was charged with criminal trespass, criminal mischief, and attempted escape after police located him passed out amid shattered glass on the floor of the Starfire restaurant. A passerby witnessed him break through the front door glass and enter. In route to the police department, handcuffed in the rear seat, suspect tried to climb out a rear patrol car window.

08/10/13: Harbor personnel called and reported that a vehicle and a boat trailer were parked on the flats at the small boat harbor, with no owner in sight and the tide coming in. Officer responded and unlocked the vehicle so that it could pulled to safer area.

08/10/13: A tour operator reported to police that he had pulled his bus over near Tutshi Lake on the Klondike Highway to watch a moose cross the road. As his passengers watched in horror, a vehicle heading toward Skagway at a high rate of speed struck the moose, hurling it over the top of the car. Police located the damaged vehicle in a rental lot.

08/11/13: Police contacted a couple tent camping in the trees on the north side of the school. They were advised that the school property is a no-camping zone.

08/11/13: Police were dispatched to investigate a large cloud of smoke on Broadway. The smoke was traced to a restaurant, and the chef advised that 24 burgers at a time on the grill will do that.

08/11/13: Police received a noise complaint of a headlamp wearing man mowing his Main Street lawn after 10 p.m. Officers arrived to the smell of freshly cut grass, however the man had finished his chores.

2013

08/13/13: A Skagway man reported he had either lost or had his wallet stolen. Checking, he found that his debit card had been used to the tune of $300 at three different local bars the night before.

08/16/13: Police responded to a vehicle vs. fire hydrant collision on Fourth Avenue. Vehicle took the brunt of the damage.

08/20/13: A visitor told police he believes that his wallet was pick-pocketed, emptied of a $100 bill and then slipped back into his pocket.

08/22/13: Police found an intoxicated bicyclist crashed on State Street. The man could barely talk, stand, or walk, and agreed to be taken into protective custody for the night.

08/22/13: A local man threatened violence against a business for refusing to allow him and his service dog into the business. Business said man was not allowed on property with or without the animal after allegedly harassing store clerks.

08/27/13: Business reported $400 of clothing shoplifted. Two suspects visible on a security camera were identified after a photo was posted of Facebook. Officers are working on securing a warrant for the pair.

08/29/13: Police investigated an altercation and disturbance over whether or not one party had made a clandestine video of another during a hook-up encounter.

09/07/13: An injured crow was reported to have stumbled into a jewelry store.

09/08/13: Police monitored flooding in Dyea, gathered requested information and photographs for NOAA. Weather service advising this appears to be third highest river level recorded on Taiya River.

09/25/13: Police assisted USCG by providing alcohol breath tests to seven crew members after a tug boat and an ore ship collided, leaving a hole in the ore ship.

09/27/13: Police located a highly intoxicated individual lying under the bushes near 12th and Main Street. In an attempt to take the man home, police drove to four different addresses before the man remembered where he lived.

Best of the Skagway Police Blotter

11/15/13: Police were called for a man passed out and lying on the 18-degree ground. After waking the man, police had him checked out by EMS before taking him home.

11/23/13: A 49-year-old Skagway man was transported to Lemon Creek Correctional Center and held on $10,000 bail after being charged with felony assault. He was accused of shooting his roommate with a 12-gauge shotgun in a bedroom of their Spring Street home. Victim was medevaced to hospitals in Juneau and then Seattle, suffering from a blast-shattered shoulder.

11/24/13: An extremely intoxicated individual repeatedly called 911 to report he was locked inside somewhere, but couldn't tell where. Police and friends searched the area around his residence where he was finally located – inside a locked storage shed – and returned home.

12/04/13: Police responding to a reported fight on Spring Street instead found workers from the city and AP&T noisily trying to corral water from a main valve break flooding the area.

12/05/13: Baby Jesus was reportedly stolen from manger scene at Presbyterian Church. Baby was secured into crib this year to keep from blowing away as happened last year.

12/10/13: Police investigated a one-car, non-injury, rollover traffic collision on the Klondike Highway. Police cited the 62-year-old Skagway driver for driving with an expired drivers license and driving without proof of insurance.

12/12/13: A local resident reported that an envelope of prescription medicine was missing. The medication was delivered to the Juneau airport by a Juneau pharmacy, however according to the airlines the medication never arrived in Skagway. Juneau police are also investigating the disappearance.

12/17/13: Police found a plastic grocery bag lying on Broadway Street containing a set of keys, prescription glasses, and a satellite TV remote control marked "WEST." A Broadway Street resident saw a photo of the items on the PD's Facebook page and claimed the keys and glasses, however he said the TV remote was not his.

12/31/13: A "very heavy" 5-gallon money jar about half full with change and bills was reported stolen from a 21st Avenue residence. Police investigation pointed to a family member who knew the jar's whereabouts.

2014

Cat brawlers, PD vehicle rampage, repeat bicycle stealers, campers on public property, Yukon girls gone wild for cruisers, and a very busy bear year downtown.

01/13/14: A $600 satellite phone was reported stolen from a Whitehorse school bus. The bus was in town for a basketball tournament.

01/28/14: Police received a report of an aggressive male black and white cat repeatedly fighting with area pets near Seventh and Alaska Street. The caller advised she had been scratched trying to break up a fight.

02/16/14: Police were called for a man and dog staying in a motel room who were not registered guests. Police removed the man, who had just been banned from Canada for possessing a handgun in his vehicle. The man claimed the resulting $500 fine had left him indigent. Police purchased him a ferry ticket to Juneau and escorted him aboard.

03/05/14: Police and Fire responded to an out-of-control fire among construction debris piled in a construction yard near Milepost 3 on the Klondike Highway. Complaints of smoke were received by dispatch as far south as Second and Main Street. A partial evacuation of nearby residents west of the Skagway River was started due to the possible toxic nature of the heavy black smoke. Evacuees were asked to stay away from their homes and businesses for about an hour until the fire was controlled and extinguished.

Best of the Skagway Police Blotter

03/07/14: Police received a report of a commercial vehicle stolen from downtown. A public works employee watching for the rig discovered it…downtown, where the driver had forgotten he had parked it.

03/27/14: Police contacted an individual with an extensive (pages) of criminal history who hitch-hiked into town today. Police assisted the traveler with exploring various opportunities to leave town.

04/02/14: Police investigated a report of a possible impaired driver on Dyea Road. Police made contact and determined the driver was a beginner learning how to drive.

04/08/14: A store clerk reported that an indigent-looking seasonal worker had bought two bottles of vodka with old silver coins. When officers reviewed the surveillance video they recognized the customer as a probationer who was prohibited from possessing alcohol. The 48-year-old man was contacted at his residence and arrested for probation violations.

04/13/14: Police received a theft report of a missing quartz crystal valued at $500. The rock is about 20" long and 6" wide, clear to white with one polished face, and was last seen last fall outside a Broadway Street business.

04/16/14: A Haines resident reported his boat trailer which he had left at Liarsville was missing. Police located and contacted a local man who had thought the trailer had been abandoned. Trailer was returned to the complainant.

04/18/14: Police suggested alternative locations to campers who had pitched a tent in the grass next to City Hall.

04/27/14: Police responded to a reported thrown glass possibly striking a vehicle and a disturbance at a downtown bar. Suspect was gone on arrival, business decided to close for the night. Police appreciated discretion shown by staff in closing.

GRAD STYLIN' – The Skagway High School Class of 2014, all four of them, showed up for their outdoor graduation ceremony in a nice ride, courtesy of local auto restorer Tobias Parsons.

– Katie Emmets

04/27/14: Police received a complaint of a car parked on the sidewalk and tent campers inside a closed campground on Congress Way. Police contacted the campers, who said they were too intoxicated to drive home after the beer festival.

04/30/14: Police received a report that numerous grave markers at the pet cemetery had been pulled up. Officers collected and tried to match the markers to the best of their ability to existing holes in the ground and restore the area.

05/01/14: Police stopped the driver of a pickup truck for having passengers in the bed and riding on a tailgate. The driver appeared intoxicated to the officer, and failed several field sobriety tests. He was transported to the station where he blew a .16 BAC. The 21-year-old seasonal worker was arrested for driving under the influence of alcohol. Because he had a prior DUI conviction from Idaho in 2010 he was held over until court.

Best of the Skagway Police Blotter

05/07/14: A caller reported it appeared a man had just flattened tires on vehicles at the police chief's house, and then stole a bicycle from the caller's yard and was escaping northbound on Main Street. The on-duty officer confirmed the flat tires at the chief's house, and while searching for the suspect found flat tires on a patrol car and personal car of an officer living on 19th Avenue. Dispatch then called out all available officers, as it appeared someone was disabling patrol cars, and called out the Fire Department after she noticed her car ablaze in the police department parking lot. An intensive search resulted in the arrest of a 21-year-old seasonal worker on suspicion of slashing and flattening 29 vehicle tires around town, including disabling three city police patrol vehicles, setting a police dispatcher's vehicle afire, assaulting a police officer, egging the police chief's house, bicycle theft, and violating the conditions of release for the DUI arrest of 05/01. He was transported to Lemon Creek Correctional Center in Juneau.

05/13/14: An officer stopped a vehicle for having a broken taillight and an expired registration. The 34-year-old Skagway driver appeared intoxicated, and failing field tests was transported to the police department. He was cited for DUI and refusing to submit to a chemical test, released on his own recognizance, and provided a ride home.

05/15/14: An officer stopped a vehicle for erratic driving and speeding. The 44-year-old Ketchikan driver appeared intoxicated, and failing field tests was transported to the police department. He was cited for DUI and refusing to submit to a chemical test, released on his own recognizance, and provided a ride home.

05/15/14: Police investigated a hit and run traffic collision in which a car struck a bicycle rack and drove it into the metal siding of Fairway Market. Police discovered the damaged vehicle responsible on 21st Avenue. A 66-year-old Skagway man was charged with driving on a suspended driver's license, driving without insurance, and driving with an expired vehicle registration.

05/16/14: Police responded to a possible bear sighting near 19th Avenue. Caller later decided noise had come from neighbor putting out their garbage.

05/16/14: Police re-directed a tent camper from the lawn of City Hall.

2014

05/17/14: An officer observed a person steal a bike from a bike rack on Fifth Avenue, and confiscated him after he dumped the bike near Spring Street. The officer took the suspect back to his campsite. Officer returned to collect the bike and found it had been stolen again.

05/17/14: Police asked residents to cease dropping or throwing water balloons from the roof of the hardware store onto pedestrians.

05/18/14: Police received a report of a "couple of large blood stains" on the pavement on State Street near the Rec Center.

05/18/14: Dispatch received a 911 call from a child advising that his sister and brother were stuck on their deck and couldn't get down. The 4-year-old hung up, but called back a few minutes later and asked if anybody was coming to help. Dispatch was able to then talk to child's parents, who advised everything was fine and no police response was needed.

05/19/14: Police coned off a large rock that had rolled into the lane of travel on Dyea Road near Long Bay. Several trees had accompanied the rock, and about 150 feet of bank above the roadway appeared unstable.

05/20/14: Police were advised that a "rough looking" man, not a passenger, had tried to board a cruise ship at the Broadway Dock and had been turned away by ship security.

05/21/14: Police picked up an intoxicated woman lying on the white line of the Klondike Highway near DOT shops, and attempted to give her a ride home, although it took 20 minutes and two mistaken addresses before she remembered where she lived.

05/26/14: A charter operator, on his boat in the small boat harbor, called police when he observed two individuals attempting to steal bikes from the bike rack. Police contacted both thieves in the harbor parking lot. They said they thought the bikes had been "abandoned." Police made sure they were clear with the concept of "stealing," and both promised to lay low and stay out of trouble until they leave town in the morning.

Best of the Skagway Police Blotter

05/31/14: A local man was driven to the police station by a friend, where he reported he had been assaulted by his live-in girlfriend in their residence after a night of drinking. The 34-year-old suspect was home and arrested without incident on a domestic violence assault charge.

06/02/14: Police asked a couple found tent camping in the Gold Rush Cemetery to set up camp elsewhere.

06/04/14: Police responded to a reported assault between a man and a woman on Third Avenue. Although witnesses reported seeing the man punch the woman in her face, neither party, both cruise ship passengers, wanted to cooperate with police. Police took female half back to her ship and advised ship security of the call. Male half, who had been drinking, was advised to walk back to the ship.

06/09/14: Dispatch received a report of an injured juvenile crow on the boardwalk "surrounded by 30 other crows."

06/11/14: Police contacted three highly intoxicated crew members reportedly fighting at Pullen Park. All three were escorted back to their ship. One combatant needed to be subdued, and was transported back onto the ship in a wheelchair by security officers.

06/11/14: Haines PD advised Skagway PD of a 911 call they received from a lost hiker at Sturgill's Landing. His cruise ship agreed to stay in port an extra half hour while Search and Rescue and the cruise ship agent worked to get him off the trail and back to his ship.

06/12/14: A 38-year-old seasonal worker was arrested for domestic violence assault for threatening his roommates and putting them in fear. Later police also served two DV protection orders on him on behalf of his roommates.

06/13/14: Police located and walked down with an elderly hiker making his way after midnight from Upper Lake and the Devil's Punchbowl. The visitor from Florida had not been aware what toll the downhill trek was going to take on his knees.

2014

06/17/14: Police helped transport an intoxicated individual found passed out on the ground back to their Fifth Avenue residence.

06/22/14: Police furnished courtesy rides to several intoxicated individuals after festivities.

06/22/14: Police contacted an intoxicated bicycle rider who kicked over several traffic cones on State Street. Police asked her to put them back.

06/26/14: Police opened a vehicle stuck on the Dyea tide flats in which the owner had locked her keys and her dog inside.

06/26/14: Police were unable to get a highly intoxicated man up from lying in an alley. Police, EMS and the subject's mother finally got him on his feet and lugged home.

06/29/14: Police were called when the soon-to-be-groom in a Whitehorse wedding party passed out on a downtown boardwalk and could not get back up. Groom was stuffed in rear of patrol car and transported with a member of the party to a Dyea Road residence where he was maneuvered inside for the night.

06/29/14: Police contacted a late night coach cleaning crew who were having too much fun cleaning and consequently disturbing the neighbors.

07/01/14: Police responded to a business complaint on one store by another. Complaining store was upset other store was advertising "70% off sale." Officer advised that sign is legal; only "end of season" signs are illegal before Labor Day.

07/01/14: A local resident turned over to police a black pouch that was picked up off the road. They saw it fall from the roof of a vehicle and were going to try and catch up and return it, until they noticed the pouch contained a quantity of marijuana and a wood pipe. Pouch's owner has not contacted police to reclaim it.

Best of the Skagway Police Blotter

WORTHY DUNKING – Members of the Skagway Borough Assembly took the ALS Ice Bucket Challenge after an August 2014 work session. They were challenged by students of the Skagway School's fifth and sixth grade classes, and they subsequently challenged the Haines Borough Assembly. During the challenge, the assembly discussed how the disease has hit home, with three residents dying from ALS in the last ten years. The ALS Challenge swept up social media that summer and at this point had raised more than $94.3 million in just a couple of weeks.

07/03/14: Police received three calls of a recklessly driven Yukon-plated vehicle on the north end of town. Police located the vehicle and a Whitehorse area driver and passenger in the car. These ladies also had two male cruise ship members in the back seat. The cruise ship was waiting to untie and depart and was only awaiting the return of their missing crew. An officer gave the members a courtesy ride back to ship security, and another gave the girls a courtesy escort out of the country.

07/04/14: Police stopped a fight downtown between an intoxicated local man and three intoxicated visitors. Local man did not approve of the shirt a visitor was wearing and tried to tear it off of him. Man was given a courtesy ride home.

07/05/14: Police watched an early morning driver make a hard turn and then park in the lane of travel after the driver noticed the patrol car behind them. Officer drove around the block and watched as the driver and a passenger jumped out and hurriedly switched places. Occupants could not give the officer a reasonable explanation for their actions after contact was made. Occupants agreed to surrender their IDs and car keys and walk home for the night.

07/05/14: Visitors using the overflow camping area reported that part of the group had scattered beer cans throughout the area and were using the bushes to relieve themselves. Reporting party was afraid the few would wreck the hospitality shown to the many.

2014

07/06/14: Dispatch took a report that someone had apparently "taken a dump" on a walkway between two downtown businesses. Caller wanted police to watch out for similar behavior.

07/07/14: Users of Mollie Walsh Park found hitting the bottle were asked to pour out the contents of said bottles and warned not drink intoxicants in public in the Historic District.

07/07/14: Police took a traffic collision report from an adult bicycle rider who complained that a pack of young girl cyclists had not only struck her bike, knocking her to the ground, but also ran her over. The next day police took a report from four young girls advising that an adult on a bike had run into them, causing an accident, and then kicked and assaulted one of the girls.

07/08/14: A Good Samaritan brought to the police station a young man found stranded in Dyea. The man had been traveling with his father from Toronto, but when the father became upset he kicked the young man out of the car and drove off. Dispatch was able to contact the man's mother, and a second Good Samaritan gave him a lift to Whitehorse to catch a flight home.

07/15/14: Piling insult upon injury, a bicycle reported stolen was found in the Skagway River, apparently thrown from the footbridge.

07/15/14: A local employer told police that they were concerned about a disgruntled ex-employee. Employer had shipped the man's belongings – including a handgun – to him in Juneau. Employee claimed a garnet was missing, and he would be returning to Skagway "to tear the place apart" until he found his gem.

07/24/14: U.S. Customs called police requesting a courtesy ride for a man who had walked from town to Fraser and back after being refused entry into Canada.

07/29/14: Police received a call about a homeless man with no ID trying to secure a hotel room. Police found the man, the same one who had been refused entry to Canada, and got him some coffee and a place to get out of the rain.

Best of the Skagway Police Blotter

07/31/14: An Alaska Street resident photographed a man stealing her neighbor's bicycle. Photos were put on Facebook and sent to police. Locals caught the suspect near the Skagway River Bridge and held him for police. The 20-year-old Tacoma, WA man was arrested and held overnight on theft charges.

08/05/14: Police contacted two visitors downtown who were reportedly intoxicated and harassing people. They were given a ride back to their cruise ship, and police notified ship security of their condition.

08/06/14: Police confiscated a blue Ozark Trail tent, a backpack and various other items abandoned on the Lower Lake Trail. Property apparently belongs to homeless man in town the week before.

08/10/14: Police received a report of a larger than usual, more intoxicated than usual, group of bear watchers practicing unsafe gazing at the Dyea Flats.

08/12/14: A woman managed to get bear spray on her face. She declined an ambulance, and friends drove her to the clinic.

08/12/14: While investigating yelling and screaming, police found three people sitting and drinking inside the locomotive near City Hall. They agreed to clean up their mess and call it a night.

08/13/14: Police received a complaint of naked men riding on the roof of an SUV.

08/15/14: Police responded to an assault occurring near the dike off 21st and Alaska Street. A verbal argument reportedly escalated after one man knocked another to the ground. The standing man threatened to strike the lying man, until the lying man pulled a handgun on the standing man, telling him to back off. The standing man did so, and the two retreated to their respected residences.

08/16/14: Another sign Skagway is safe and secure: after a patron fell through a window of the Red Onion, the window was secured for the night with a piece of cardboard. Business and contents remained safe behind the paper barrier until new glass was installed the next morning.

08/17/14: A 49-year-old Skagway man was arrested (again) and held on probation violations (again) after a visiting state probation officer found him at his residence in possession or consumption of alcohol (again) and marijuana.

08/22/14: EMS transported an unconscious intoxicated woman from the boardwalk near Seventh Avenue to the clinic. Police then transferred woman home after treatment.

08/23/14: Police contacted a man sleeping inside the post office. He is supposed to leave on the ferry today, and will wait at the ferry terminal instead. Police were called to the terminal a couple of hours later when the man was reportedly causing a ruckus there.

08/23/14: Police contacted an intoxicated man relieving himself in a parking lot, and took his vehicle keys from him until morning.

08/25/14: A man without proper ID reportedly tried to gain access to two cruise ships.

08/25/14: Police chased a large black bear off the Railroad Dock.

08/29/14: Police contacted an assault victim and suspect outside a downtown bar. The suspect had reportedly punched the victim in the face over a perceived slight toward a woman. Victim did not want to press charges, and police separated the parties.

08/29/14: Police investigated a death aboard the Carnival Miracle. Victim, a 49-year-old Virginia man died of apparent natural causes.

09/01/14: A bear was reported seen near 20th and Alaska.

09/05/14: A large brown bear was reported near Dyea Road and the Klondike Highway.

Best of the Skagway Police Blotter

09/06/14: A large brown bear was reported in Seven Pastures.

09/08/14: Police harassed a bear away from Seven Pastures.

09/12/14: A bear was reported near 15th and Main, 20th and Alaska, swimming across the river toward Seven Pastures, on Dyea Road, and on 18th heading toward the railroad tracks.

09/12/14: Police checked on a man sleeping on the grass parking strip near 10th and Broadway. He had made it from an employee party to within a few blocks of home before passing out. A friend agreed to walk him the rest of the way.

09/13/14: Police gave numerous courtesy rides home to pedestrians either too tipsy to efficiently walk home, or concerned about the number of bear sightings.

09/14/14: Police responded to the Corner Gas Station after a German customer driving a rental car drove off with the gas nozzle still inside the filler hole. Gas hose was torn from pump, causing a reported $2,500 damage, however no fuel was spilled.

09/14/14: A found wallet containing a Texas driver's license, money, student ID, a port security card, and a false ID indicating the holder was over 21 was turned over to police. Officers called the owner and offered that he could come down and claim it, however he left town the next day without picking it up instead.

09/14/14: A 18-year-old Kentucky woman was held overnight on an outstanding arrest warrant at the request of the Fayette County (KY) Sheriff Department.

09/14/14: A bear was reported near the railroad tracks on the north end of town.

09/15/14: Police contacted a female kicked out of employee housing by her employer in the middle of the night for disruptive behavior. She and her possessions were given a courtesy ride to a friend who took her in.

2014

09/15/14: Police were unable to stop a suspected intoxicated driver driving an ATV. An officer waited at his residence after losing him atop the river dike; however the suspect hid in the trees across from his Klondike Highway residence and declined to come home.

09/16/14: Police offered a ride home to an intoxicated bicyclist who had crashed near 10th and Main. Cyclist only knew her first name, and after driving around several blocks without finding her house, she was dropped back off at her request to continue to push her bike "home."

09/17/14: Police checked on a bear reportedly agitated by being unable to find its way out of the fenced Alaska Marine Lines yard. Police located the bear near the waterfront and herded it out of town. Police received a report of a bear crossing Broadway Street heading toward City Hall, and a report of a bear breaking down a fence in a residential yard near Eighth and Alaska.

09/18/14: Police chased a small black bear down 18th Avenue and into the woods. Another bear was reported at Seven Pastures.

09/22/14: Police received a complaint that on August 16 a pedestrian was struck and knocked over by a vehicle driven by a Utah man at Second and Broadway. The victim and the driver exchanged information, however the victim didn't want to miss his cruise ship departure so he failed to report it at the time.

09/23/14: Police chased a brown bear back across the river after eating apples in a yard.

09/24/14: Police helped a cruise ship passenger retrace his steps and locate a wallet he dropped along a walk to the Gold Rush Cemetery.

9/25/14: Police contacted individuals who had been flying a remote control drone helicopter past the security barriers and near the cruise ships.

09/27/14: Police contacted a residence at Sixth and Main about fireworks annoying the neighborhood. All was quiet at the scene; the intoxicated pyrotechnician had passed out before officer arrival.

Best of the Skagway Police Blotter

09/28/14: Police gave an uncooperative intoxicated patron a ride home to his Broadway Street residence from a downtown establishment.

09/28/14: Police asked a group of intoxicated patrons gathered outside a downtown establishment and annoying their neighbors to take their partying back inside.

09/28/14: Police received a report of a woman stealing a bottle of wine from the liquor store. Friends of the suspect walked her and the wine back to the store before officer arrival.

09/29/14: Two men, one armed with an assault rifle, reportedly made threats toward people working on a power line in Dyea.

10/01/14: Police hazed a bear with cracker rounds off of 19th Avenue and into the woods. Another bear was reported in the alley between 11th and 12th.

10/02/14: Police received a report of a bear near 18th and Alaska Street.

10/03/14: A bear reportedly damaged Dumpsters near Fifth and Alaska Street. A bear reportedly damaged a barbecue grill, a burn barrel and a garbage can at a residence near 10th and Alaska. Another bear was reported in the alley between Seventh and Eighth streets.

10/04/14: A bear was reported near 10th and State Street.

10/05/14: Police responded to a reported intoxicated man lying in the roadway near 12th and Main Street. The man was given a courtesy ride to his residence on the Klondike Highway.

10/05/14: A bear was reported near Seven Pastures. A bear scattered garbage from several residences in the alley between 19th and 20th Avenues.

10/06/14: Police hazed a large brown bear with cracker rounds in the alley between 13th and 14th Avenues. A bear reportedly knocked over Dumpsters full of garbage near 14th and State Street. A bear reportedly tipped over a Dumpster near 15th and Main.

10/07/14: A bear reportedly tipped over a Dumpster in Mountain View campground. Police received several calls of a bear prowling around full dumpsters near 12th and Broadway. Police were able to haze the bear with a rubber bullet.

10/07/14: Police received a report that a former employee may have vandalized the sprinkler system at a business, potentially causing a malfunction. System was restored by a contractor.

10/08/14: A bear was reported in a yard on Liarsville Road. Resident reported it moved off prior to police arrival. Bears were reported near 12th and Alaska, near Sixth and Main, and near 12th and Broadway streets.

10/09/14: An 11th Avenue resident reported a bear trampled her empty garbage can.

10/10/14: Police received many calls of bear sightings between Ninth and 12th avenues. Police located many battered cans and ravished garbage spills in alleys, and chased the bear off of a few in-progress banquets.

BOTHERSOME BRUIN – A young grizzly bear takes a break from fishing to cruise through a Dyea yard. He left after eating an apple. – *Dirk Foss*

10/10/14: Police received a 911 call from the girlfriend of a 46-year-old Skagway man who said she had been assaulted by him and was hiding in a restaurant restroom. Responding officer escorted her to safety and located the suspect who was arrested on felony domestic violence assault charges and held at the request of his probation officer on state and federal violations.

10/11 to 10/13/14: Police received two reports of a bear prowling a Dumpster off Broadway Street. Another bear ran off toward the railroad tracks after another resident yelled at it. A bear was reported in a yard near 10th and Alaska and the next day near Ninth and Spring. A Dumpster was reported tipped over near Seventh and Broadway, and also at Second and Alaska. Bear sightings were reported near the school parking lot, near City Hall, and near the post office.

Best of the Skagway Police Blotter

10/16/14: An Alaska Street resident reported a bear got in his open garage and attempted to drag out his freezer. Resident scared off the bear with a blast from his air horn.

10/18/14: A bear was reported knocking over a Dumpster near Sixth and Broadway Street.

10/27/14: Police received a report that a bear had tipped a Dumpster near Second Avenue, and that the mess had been cleaned up by the owner. Police observed garbage had been strewn down an alley near Fourth and Spring. Trash was later cleaned up by owner.

10/30/14: A hide from a locally shot brown bear was sealed for state Fish and Game.

November and the first half of December was quiet in Skagway, and the blotter noted that the police, fire and EMS departments hope that this ambience of peace in the valley persists.

12/13/14: A concerned citizen staying at a local motel reported watching an apparently intoxicated man bang for several minutes on the front door of the house across the street, before forcing his way inside. Responding officers located a 48-year-old Skagway man hiding in a back bedroom, where he was arrested on a domestic violence charge.

12/16/14: A 12th Avenue resident reported someone wearing a headlamp was looking under and in the bed of a pickup parked in her yard. The man ran off when the owner walked outside.

12/27/14: Police took a report of threatening text messages. Police contacted the sending party and warned him against continued harassment.

12/28/14: While on patrol an officer noticed a large section of perimeter fence was missing at the airport, and vehicle parts were scattered 60 feet into the tarmac. The officer was able to match the parts to a damaged vehicle parked on Fourth Avenue, and located and charged a 35-year-old Skagway woman with negligent driving and failure to report a traffic accident.

Heard on the Wind

A final round of quintessential quotations from our visitors

A lady called the visitor center in February for a relocation packet.
She said she was wondering what "Ho for the Klondike" meant.
She was assured that it was not a call for a certain profession to come to the Klondike. – 04/27/12

In a Florida article mailed to a newsie, someone mentioned that they were going to Alaska. The writer then commented, "It's so far up there, it's like a different country. I'm surprised they speak English." – 05/11/12

A woman coming off one of this year's first cruise ships at the Broadway Dock looked over the railing at the water spilling into the bay from the Pullen Creek salmon ladder, 20 feet below, and said, "I wonder if I can pan for gold in there." – 05/11/12

At the start of the day in the bank, people were in line, teller windows were staffed, and all of the banking staff were in their places, when a lady walked in and, in a surprised way, exclaimed, "Is this a real bank?" – 05/25/12

The new bike patrol officer was asked if the reason police officers rode bikes was because the town could not afford to give them police cars. – 05/25/12

A TEMSCO helicopter was seen hauling a sling-load of provisions up to Glacier Station. A visitor asked, "Do they always take people up hanging on a rope?" – 05/25/12

A visitor asked where they could get an item, while pointing at a picture in a coupon book. The retail employee said, "That's in Ketchikan."
The tourist replied, "Where is that store?" – 05/25/12

A newcomer to Alaska was on a tour and asked about the flora and fauna. At one point the guide talked about Rubus Spectabilis, aka Salmonberry, to which the very nice but not overly bright lady responded, "Alaskan salmon eat berries? How do they jump that high?" – 05/25/12

The train whistle tooted and a woman said, "Bless you!" – 06/08/12

POLITICALLY INCORRECT – Those Sarah Palin questions were so incessant for a while that some locals took to the streets to mock the beleaguered ex-governor during the Fourth of July parade in 2010.

At the visitor center, a lady asked who could join the Arctic Brotherhood.

She was told "Stampeders."

She then asked "Why could horses join? Did they stampede down the street?" – 06/22/12

At the M&M tour shack by the Railroad Dock, a woman came in with her husband and two children and asked about the train trip.

The tour broker showed her the route on a map all the way up past the White Pass summit and the international boundary.

The lady then asked, "Is that Russia?

The tour broker looked her straight in the eye and stated, "No ma'am, it's Canada?"

But they were still confused.

Another person at the same shack later in the week asked, "How far is Russia from here?"

When told by the tour seller that it was about 2,500 miles, the visitor responded, "Then I guess we can't see it from here."

This drew a very grim reaction from the tour shack attendants.

The visitor, sensing the obvious, stated, "I didn't want to bring up Sarah Palin, but…"

"It's better that you didn't." – 06/22/12

Expecting to see members of the "Vampire Cruise," someone asked a friend where all the vampires were. He suggested that the vampires must be in their coffins on board the ship since it's always daytime in Alaska at this time of year. – 07/13/12

An agitated man comes into the visitor center and points at the Alaska map, points to the Aleutian Chain and demands to know which islands President Obama has given away to Russia. He is told that is not so. A little research revealed it was President George H.W. Bush, who signed a 1991 treaty with Russia permanently establishing a maritime boundary with that country, putting seven islands off the Kamchatka Peninsula and Russia's northern coast on Russia's side. The State Department states no U.S. claims have ever been made for the islands. – 07/13/12

Overhead on the boardwalk: "There's got to be casinos here. That's why there are so many tour buses." – 07/13/12

A couple came into the visitor center and asked for things to do after leaving the NPS walking tour because there was "too much walking." – 07/27/12

"Where can you take the ferry to Russia?" a customer asked in the Russian American Co. store.
– 07/27/12

Some risqué wind from the street madames at the RO...
A visitor walked up to a madame and asked, "Don't you know those things are for breastfeeding?!" The madame looked down, and looked up, "Do you know Jesus is your Lord and Saviour?" Another gentleman said to a madame who was standing in the rain, "Aren't you getting all wet?" "Yes sir!" the madame replied. "It's part of my job and I'm good at it!" – 08/10/12

A woman looking toward a glacier remarked, "Oh look, there's a glacier. What a pretty color it is." Her husband agreed, and said, "That blue color means it's a new one." – 08/10/12

A man walking down the boardwalk noticed a SMART shuttle bus with its doors open. Then a crow walked up to the open door, crouching like it was ready to jump inside the bus, and the driver shut the door and drove off.
"No free rides," remarked the man to the crow.
Another man who had been watching the episode chimed in, "I guess he didn't have two bucks."
– 08/10/12

HEARD ON THE WIND

A lady came into the visitor center and asked if there were any stores where you could just go in and buy things. – 08/24/12

A river guide pointed out the rounded river rocks on the Taiya's shoreline. He was then asked, "Who brought them in and put them there?" – 08/24/12

A nice Whitehorse couple stopped in for some cup cakes and asked, "When did it start getting so windy here?"

"Well…since it was a valley," the proprietor replied.

"Oh no," one of the visitors replied. "We've been here before. It's never been this windy." – 09/14/12

"Are you having a drought?" asked a man with a Texas twang.

"No, in fact it's been the rainiest summer I've seen in many years," replied the local.

"Well then, why is the water so low in the lake? We noticed that when our ship came in." – 09/14/12

A guide was talking about the omnivorous diet of bears and a great series of photos that a local photographer took of a bear that came out of the bush and killed two helpless kids while its mother, the nanny watched. The horrified visitor asked what she did, and was even more horrified to learn that she sold copies of the photos around town. It soon became obvious that the New Yorker was more familiar with a nanny and kids in the city, and not a mountain goat family in the wilds of our mountains.

– 09/14/12

During the famous "Soap Pitch" by Soapy Smith in the Days of '98 Show, an audience member yelled, "They give us all the free soap we want on the ship." – 09/14/12

"Is this the real town of Skagway, or is the real town somewhere else?"– 09/28/12

A woman with a lesbian tour group off a ship asked a train guide what the store Dejon Delights sold.

"They sell smoked salmon," the guide said.

"Oh s--t!" the woman exclaimed.

"What did you think they sold?" asked the guide.

"I was hoping it was a pleasure store. We missed the one in Juneau!" – 09/28/12

Two men walk off a ship at the Broadway Dock and notice the fish ladder spilling water from Pullen

HEARD ON THE WIND

Creek into the bay. One man asks the other, "Are there signs that tell them where to jump?" – 05/24/13

Customer: "Do you have this shirt in a 3XL?
Store clerk: "No, I'm sorry. The largest size we carry is a 2XL in that shirt."
Customer: "What?! Isn't this America?" – 05/24/13

"Where are your penguins?" a visitor asked. "I 'Googled' before we left and it said you have them all over Alaska." – 06/14/13

A tourist approached a sales clerk at the Skagway Mining Co. and asked if they had any brown polar bears.
"We can roll one in the dirt," commented the clerk, and the visitor just looked confused. – 06/14/13

A man on a bus tour looked over "Tormented Valley" and said, "Do you think they brought these rocks in, or are they natural?" – 06/14/13

A woman came into a restaurant and asked, "Where can I go to see the iceberg that sank the Titanic?"
– 06/14/13

A man called the Northern Lights Pizzeria and said, "Northern Lights?"
The manager answered, "Yes, it is."
The man then said, "What time do you turn on the Northern Lights?"
Manager (laughing): "I usually flip the switch at 11:15."
Man: "Okay." And hangs up. – 06/14/13

"I want to go swimming with the orcas…you know, like the dolphins in Florida. How come they don't have that here?" – 06/28/13

A dog tied up next to The Sweet Tooth Cafe was howling for its owner when a woman walking on Broadway Street turned to her husband with a terrified look and said "See! I knew we would have to worry about wolves in Alaska towns!" – 06/28/13

A couple was sitting on the rocks at Yakutania Point, and the woman asked her companion, "Do you think we can see the ocean from here?" – 07/12/13

HEARD ON THE WIND

A suggestion heard at the museum: "Haines is known for strawberries and Skagway has lots of rhubarb - you guys should get together and have a jam!" – 07/12/13

"Why is it light here?" a visitor asked a park interpreter. "I heard it was the 'Land of the Midnight Sun' and expected it to be light at night and dark during the day." – 07/12/13

A woman came into the visitor center and asked, in all seriousness: "Where are the jewelry stores? I haven't seen any."
When told to just continue down the street and she would find several jewelry stores, she then asked, "Do they sell earrings?"
And then, after one of them found what they were looking for, they too were perplexed:
"Why doesn't your McDonald's have the double arches?"
Upon being informed that the red and yellow building was a jewelry store, the visitor asked, "Do you have any other good restaurants like that here?" – 07/12/13

A customer at the Klothes Rush was seen looking at the "Isn't Texas Cute?" shirt with the state of Texas inside the state of Alaska. He looked confused and shocked.
"Is this true?" he asked.
"Yes," the clerk replied. "Alaska is bigger than Texas."
Still shocked, the man looked at his wife and asked, "Did you know this, honey?"
Equally shocked, she said, "No, I'm just learning this like you!"
"I can't believe this!" the man exclaimed.
The clerk applied the finishing blow: "Yes, my state is bigger than yours." – 07/26/13

More questions from the VC:
"Why is it so hot here?"
"Where is the Costco?"
"Is this Whitehorse?"
"It's so weird because we are in Alaska, but we are also in America?"
"What is hiking?"
"Do you have the 'How to NOT get eaten by a bear' brochure here?"
"What happens if a grizzly bear comes closer to the coast? Do you shoot it?"
"If I throw a stick, will a bear chase it?" – 07/26/13

While on a wildlife watching tour, onlookers saw three different whales, a handful of seals, an eagle's nest, and a waterfall. After seeing such a variety, a tourist from LA looked over at the tour guide and asked, "Are we gonna see anything?" – 08/09/13

Overheard from the newsroom window: "I love this place. It's like being in a western. I keep waiting for the horse to come along." – 08/09/13

A passenger on a small bus tour asked a driver, "What are the regulations for how far you are supposed to stand away from a bear if you see one in the wild?" – 08/23/13

After being driven through town and having various employee housing buildings pointed out and then ending up at the overlook with a great view of the town, a visitor repeatedly asked, "But where do the people live?" – 08/23/13

A driver was guiding a tour out to Dyea and they stopped to watch humpback whales in Long Bay. After a while this lady turns to the guide and says, "Is that a whole whale?" – 08/23/13

A group of locals sitting outside their favorite watering hole were asked by a cruise ship visitor if they could explain to him how the trees in the canal can grow to the water and survive in salt water? The locals tried a few attempts at telling him that the trees have shallow roots and are above the high tide line, so they use fresh water. The man finally huffed off, saying "I'll find someone that can tell me the answer." – 09/13/13

"You live here in the winter? You must be married." - said to a woman who lives in Skagway year-round. – 09/13/13

Tour passenger 1: "I'm surprised Alaska is as cold as it is. It's so close to Hawaii but it's so much colder."
Tour passenger 2: "What makes you think Alaska is close to Hawaii?"
Tour passenger 1: "Well, when I went to school there was a map of the United States in the front of our classroom and in the bottom left corner there was Alaska right next to Hawaii in a little box."
– 09/13/13

A Skagway resident in her car was slowing while coming out of an alley and stopped for visitors on the sidewalk. A woman came up to her window and said, "You know, cars are not allowed in Disney World." – 09/27/13

HEARD ON THE WIND

We will finish this last round of 2013 wind with some choice blasts from our crew of dedicated newsies:

"How far up the valley is below sea level?"

"Who paints the snow on the mountains? It can't be real since it's summer."

"What do you do with the glaciers at night?"

And the Newsie responded, in all seriousness, "We unplug them." – 09/27/13

A man off one of the first ships of the season walked up to a Skaguay Alaskan newsie on the dock and asked, "Are you the mayor?"

The newsie dutifully responded, "Yes, sir!"

The visitor looked at the other newsie and said, "You must be the vice mayor, then?"

The second newsie took a little offense, and said he wanted to be the mayor.

"I can see we have a political turf war on our hands!" the visitor responded, and handed both boys a tip. – 05/09/14

Overheard on the "Doc Holiday"...

As the charter fishing boat was leaving the harbor with a group of visitors from a Princess ship, one member of the party looked up at the large white vessels to the left and asked of Captain Greg, "Are those cruise ships?" – 06/25/14

Overheard at Fifth and Broadway at rhubarb corner...

"Those are Jurassic rhubarb plants!"

And on another day, same location, observing the same plants, a very knowledgeable fellow explained: "Those are giant Alaskan cabbages." – 06/25/14

Another take on the huge rhubarb plant at Fifth and Broadway…

"Those are Swiss chard," said a confident sounding woman. – 07/11/14

A wind gatherer was walking from the post office to his car and heard, over his shoulder, "Oh, look dear. Amazon ships here too." – 07/25/14

After asking many questions about winter living in Alaska, a visitor finally asks a store clerk, "Do you get hot water?"

Confused, the staff member asks, "Do you mean natural hot springs?"

The visitor replies, "No, I mean for showers and doing dishes." – 08/15/14

HEARD ON THE WIND

A visitor was overheard stating why she would not go into the AB Hall visitor center. "I was afraid to go in. It was built with little sticks." – 08/15/14

From the SMART bus...
A Texan tells his shuttle driver they are celebrating their 45th wedding anniversary.
SMART driver says, "Wow, that's great! You bring your wife all the way to Alaska to celebrate your 45th. What you going to do for your 50th?"
The man says, "Well, I'm going to come back and get her..." – 08/15/14

Many tour ramblings...
While giving a tour, a driver stopped at Pitchfork Falls up the highway for photographs. One of the passengers remarked on the green pipe next to the falls and asked, with all sincerity, "Is that part of the Alaska Pipeline?"
On another tour earlier in the week a passenger asked, "Where can we go to see Russia?"
When the driver replied that you couldn't see Russia while visiting Skagway, the passenger said, "Well, where are Alaska and Russia attached then?"
The driver informed her they were not attached, and she said, "Well they have to be attached, the United States bought Alaska from Russia!"
The driver gave up and smiled.
Finally while driving by Summit Lake a passenger remarked, "Is that lake too shallow for whales?"
"Yes, it is," the driver said.
"But it is salt water, right?" – 08/29/14

Another whale of a tale...
The windy one and one of his ace newsies were passing out papers on the Broadway Dock and saw a seal bob up by the Pullen Creek salmon chute. They immediately pointed it out to passing visitors, with an exclamation: "Seal!"
To which a man responded, "Whale!" and ran over to look.
"No, seal!" the windy one responded.
"Seal, whale... what's the difference–" the man replied.
Dumbfounded, the two Skagway ambassadors shook their heads, and said, "Well, size, for one."
– 08/29/14

HEARD ON THE WIND

NEWSIES UNITE – The Skaguay Alaskan newsies load up on ice cream courtesy of the windy one, as they get ready for another season on the docks.

A pretty little five-year-old girl danced into a local curio shop. She was very excited. Her mother then explained that "she saw the sign on your door, she wants her free kitten."

The child had seen the sign on the door which reads, "Unattended children will be given an espresso and a free kitten." – 09/12/14

And finally, from the windy one...

On his last day on the dock for this year – a sunny one at that – the windy one was asked, "Where are all the Skags in Skagway?"

The windy one replied, "There are none. We are full of beautiful people."

And the visitor replied, "We agree, this is the most beautiful place we have seen in 25 years."

– 09/26/14

About the Authors

Dave Sexton has 30 years in law enforcement – half of those have been as a chief of police in various communities. He has spent 14 years of his career off and on in Skagway. He is a graduate of the FBI National Academy and has a Masters degree in Justice Administration from the University of Alaska Fairbanks. He likes to mix it up between patrol cars and ivory towers: he has taught at community colleges in California, Oregon and Washington and is an associate professor and program manager of law enforcement at the University of Alaska Southeast. He lives in Skagway.

Jeff Brady was the editor of The Skagway News during the period in which this book covers. He sold the paper in 2015 but still works as a newsie supervisor on the docks, presumably because he cannot let go of his duties as "the windy one." He still owns Lynn Canal Publishing and the town's bookstore, Skaguay News Depot & Books. You'll find the first Blotter book there as well, along with his historical tome, *Skagway: City of the New Century*. He lives and writes in Dyea, where he and his artist wife Dorothy operate Alderworks Alaska Writers and Artists Retreat.

Parting Shot

ALL IN THE LINE OF DUTY – Then Police Chief Dave Sexton turns his whistle over to Dutch super model Anna-Marie Goddard to direct traffic at Second and Broadway for an *Inside Sports* magazine swimsuit issue shoot. Two historic Skagway Street Car Company park buses were staged for the shoot to create a traffic jam at the Historic District's busiest intersection. The magazine photos, featuring models and stars from the TV series "Baywatch" on an Alaska cruise, appeared in the January 1998 issue. And you thought we put a bikini-clad woman on the cover just to sell books. – *Jeff Brady*